To Sarah
God bless

GW00536417

# DEEPER YET

REFLECTIONS ON LIFE IN POETRY AND PROSE

## Pauline Barnes

First published in Great Britain in 2024

Seanic Publishing
86-90 Paul Street
London
EC2A 4NE
United Kingdom

Unless otherwise indicated, Scripture quotations are from the New King James (NKJV) or the New International Version (NIV)

ISBN 978-1-3999-6127-1

The views and opinions expressed in this work are those of the author and do not necessarily reflect the views and opinions of the publisher.

British Library Cataloguing-in-Publication Data

A catalogue record for this book is available from the British Library.

# Dedication

This book of poetry and prose is dedicated to my grandchildren Isaiah and Niemah.  Also, to the countless children of varying shades, that they may grow up in a world where, in the words of Dr Martin Luther King (Jnr), 'they will not be judged by the colour of their skin, but by the content of their character.'

### Your Face

*a grandmother's prayer*

When I saw your beautiful face
My heart overflowed with love.
And as I watched you sleeping,
I knew you were a gift from God above.

*'Let the little children come to Me, and do not forbid them; for of such is the kingdom of heaven.'*
*(Matthew 19:14)*

# Acknowledgements

This book (my first baby) saw the light of day because of a faithful God and the many midwives along the way who gave me the strength to keep pushing.

For most of you, it was a kind word of encouragement which helped me to look beyond the set-backs and see the possibilities. For others, you were there on my journey, and I'll take this opportunity to mention you by name.

Marcia, my cousin and accountability partner, who encouraged me to write through my diagnosis and recovery. You were my wall for bouncing ideas around and you've never been afraid to tell me to refine my analogies. Denise, another accountability partner, who urged me to use more Bible references and even found some for me. Thank you both.

Pastor Gerry, who wanted to see how God was going to use me after my recovery. I believe this could be it Pastor!

My Esther 4 sisters – though you didn't know it – through our lively weekly discussions and prayers you were watering seeds of promise and hope.

Sister Stella, for taking me under your wings and helping me to develop the confidence to step out in faith in a number of ways. Evadney, Rosie and Simone, thank you for sharing your books with me, showing me that authorship was within my grasp.

To Beverley, who helped me organise the poems chronologically.

To Sunmi, Helen and Jess thank you for going through with a fine-tooth comb as you proofread drafts.

And to my Pastor, Deji, who encouraged and affirmed in many ways, the gift I believe God has given me.

And finally, to my family on both sides of the Atlantic, for putting up with me, by appreciating the love affair between my computer and me, and forgiving me when calls were neglected.

Thank you all, the gestation period is now over and my first book has been birthed.

To God be the glory!

# CONTENTS

## Part Two

A personal interpretation of how God reveals Himself in the 23rd Psalm

## Part Three

Prose to Ponder

Waiting for God?
Passing the Baton
Seeds of Hope Are Growing
Going Through the Fire
 Presenting the Case for an Inclusive Curriculum
I Have a Dream

# Foreword

## by Rev. Deji Ayorinde
### Lead Pastor: Pollards Hill Baptist Church
### Founding Partner: Leadership Matters Institute

I have always counted it an honour whenever I am invited to contribute something to a God-given vision, whether that is to preach in a church, provide counsel, or critique a theological essay. Providing the foreword for this book is right there at the top of the list.

Having known Pauline for a number of years, I have marvelled at her gift of creative expression and this book is a distillation of a portion of that gifting. Through poetry and prose, she paints a rather vivid portrait of her own story, pulling threads of experience from childhood to adulthood, and laying out her personality and philosophy with a sense of courageous vulnerability that such a composition would require.

Beyond this, she comments on a number of significant events in world history, unafraid to touch on subjects some may find uncomfortable, yet seeking and seeing meaning in a way that is insightful, thought-provoking and inspiriational.

And yet, right there for all to see, among the writing, page after page, section after section, is the source of her strength, the source of her wisdom, the One who has inspired this work – God.

In so many ways, this book sensitively and empathically calls us to the practice of reflection on those moments of our own experiences that may be marked by joy, pain, smiles or tears. We are reminded that there can often be more to what we see and know than meets the eye, and with each step we take, we can hold to the recognition that we are not alone – God is with us.

As you journey through the pages of this book, be prepared to be inspired and educated, to be challenged and possibly even provoked as you look again at the world in which you have lived and are living.

In the midst of contemporary society's chorus of self-reliance, comes this book's message to seek and see God in all aspects of our journey, trusting Him not only to guide us as we expolore the surface, or wade in the shallows, but to be with us when we go deeper yet.

# Preface and Author's Note

Let me start by telling you a little about myself. Before all else I am first and foremost a Christian, so as I write, I try to do so through the lens of Christianity. My faith is not a vaccine, it does not provide immunity from the realities of daily living, but it keeps me grounded when faced with adversity. As I collate this work, it appears we have emerged from the devastating clutches of the COVID 19 pandemic where to date, in the UK, hundreds of thousands have died from the virus.

The racial injustice that the Black community has suffered over decades was again brought into the limelight in April 2020, when the murder of Mr. George Floyd in the U.S. was filmed on a mobile phone and sent across the world.

I do not believe that God intends for us to live our lives in neat compartments, where one compartment has no bearing on the others. Life is not like that. We take all of ourselves into situations, so life gets messy, uncomfortable and challenging at times. As someone, therefore, who tries to live out an authentic faith, I must respond to what is happening around me. Rather than providing me with an immunity, my Christian faith gives me a perspective: a way of interpreting and understanding what I see around me daily.

So why write a book like this? Writing has become part of my worship of God and as you read through the poems in particular, you may be able to identify my valley and mountain experiences. Yes, I have been along the road some of us get the 'privilege' to travel and have come out the other side because of a faithful God.

I say 'privilege' because looking back I can see how far I've come, I can see God's hand in my life and on my life. I can see now, how what I perceived as setbacks have molded my character and have made me into a stronger woman.

Having grown up with Christian guardians I knew of God, but could not say at that time I knew God. It is only much later, when I have looked back over the course of my life, that I recognised His hand has always been on my life.

My early memories of God's saving grace include:

- Jumping off a moving bus and only spraining an ankle
- Being deliberately thrown in the river to teach me how to swim and living to tell the tale
- Running across the road and being hit by a motorcycle without being critically or badly injured
- Being invited by a friend's parents to live with them following the death of my guardian

Later in life, the challenges were many – financial, health, career, relationships. Just putting food on the table was a challenge at times, and as the bills went north my confidence went south. It was during one of these 'crisis' times in my life that I cried out to God and over the months that followed my life changed in ways I could not have imagined.

I have outlined these challenges not to elicit sympathy, as the choices I made had a direct bearing on my situation. The amazing thing in all of this, was God's faithfulness in my life even when I did not regard Him.

This publication spans years of writing, both for pleasure and as a way of responding to life. I have chosen to include both 'religious' and 'secular' writings, as I believe that God is very much interested in our secular lives and not just our spiritual lives. Our God is a God of wholeness and this was clearly demonstrated by Jesus' earthly ministry. I regard everything I do as an offering to God, and I hope and pray that all my writing reflects this.

I hope this book will challenge and provoke my readers to start conversations about God's justice and love and what it should mean to be a Christian today. As we converse, we will find that these conversations will transcend gender, racial, cultural, and economic differences. These conversations will reflect the Gospel message of love and forgiveness and will become a window into the heart of God. As we do this, healing will begin and fear will dissipate. As we stand for God, we stand for healing and after the healing, peace, love and justice will be the building blocks of our communities, our nation and our world. This is the longing of my heart.

My spirit is pregnant with a new hope and expectation about what our great God is going to do.

**Pauline Barnes**

*'I beseech you therefore, brethren, by the mercies of God, that you present your bodies a living sacrifice, holy, acceptable to God, which is your reasonable  service. And do not be conformed to this world, but be transformed by the renewing of you mind, that you may prove what is that good and acceptable and perfect will of God.'  (Romans 12:1-2)*

# PART ONE

# I know a Man Who Does

I once knew a Man who could.
I once knew a Man who did.
But what happened to me, as you'll very soon see,
Changed 'who could' and
'Who can' to 'who does'.

It started eighteen months ago,
I was feeling really low,
Contracting cold after cold,
Then getting the flu
And wondering what on earth I could do.

I took myself off to the doctors
Who carefully considered the factors,
He agreed I was ill, and he gave me some pills,
I took them and waited…and waited.

Two months went by, I was really no better,
My doctor suggested we send a letter
To a consultant no doubt,
A man of some clout,
Who would soon get to the bottom of the matter.

Tired days, sleepless nights,
Tests which gave me such a fright,
Very worried, losing weight
Yet still no appetite for the food on my plate.
It could be stress, M.E. or depression,
Cold hard facts said with little compassion.

Then one day I could take it no longer,
I needed to make myself stronger.
I went down on my knees,
I had one of these (a Bible)
And I prayed and I cried and I prayed.
So as I stand  here before you tonight,
I know it was a close fight,
But a month after praying,
Yes please listen to what I'm saying,
I knew that I'd be alright.

I once knew a man who could,
I once knew a Man who did.
But give praise to the Lord,
And I pray this strikes a chord,
I have now found the One who does.

*This poem was written in 1998 and used as a testimony at my baptism at Pollards Hill Baptist Church (PHBC) that same year.*

# Why Does God Love Us So?

Creator God, Eternal one,
Who spoke this world into being.
We simply cannot understand
Why You love us so.

You created us to love and worship You,
But from Adam we've let You down,
We moan about our lot in life;
Why do You love us so?

When we moved away from You,
Thinking we knew best,
You had Your action plan worked out;
Why do You love us so?

You sent to Earth Your only Son
To bring us back to You,
And yet He was rejected;
Why do You love us so?

The shame and pain He suffered,
The tears, the agony,
The final journey to the cross;
Why do You love us so?

Thank You is simply not enough
To express the debt we owe.
Help us  live lives which demonstrate
How much we are greatly loved.


_' Yes, I have loved you with an everlasting love;_
_Therefore with lovingkindness I have drawn you.'_
_(Jeremiah 31:3)_

_'A lively consciousness of mercies received…gives birth to_
_gratitude.'_
_(St Francis de Sales)_

# Letting Go

Do you need to let go
Of something you think dear,
So that with full assurance
To God you can draw near?

Do you need to let go
Of someone very close,
So that you can receive the blessing
From the Lord of Hosts?

Do you need to let go
Of guilt, or shame, or pride,
So that you can receive God's love
As you, in Him, abide?

Do you need to let go
Of un-forgiveness, and of hate,
So that with peace and joy and love
You can demonstrate your faith?

Do you need to let go
Of the pains that wear you down,
Of anxious thoughts that threaten to
Replace God's peace with a frown?

Do you need to let go
Of cruel things buried deep within your past,
And accept God's promise
That His love will always last?

Letting go is so difficult
As to the past we slavishly cling
Through fear and intimidation,
Or simply too weak to do anything.

But God in all His goodness
Invites us to draw near,
To let go, rise up,  put our
Trust in Him, and the plans He has for us.
To give Him our unspoken fears,
To exercise our faith,
To believe His word
'I'll be with you
To the very end of time.'

*"...Cast out the bondwoman and her son; for the son of this
bondwoman shall not be heir with my son..."   (Genesis 21:10)*

*At various times during our lives, we have had to make choices,
some of which may have enhanced or blighted our lives.
There were times in my life, when I knew the choices to make,
but because of fear I held back. I thank God that on one of
those occasions when I needed to make an important health
decision which meant a significant drop in my salary, I had the
confidence and trust in God to make the right decision. I learnt
through that experience, that we always need to just let go
because God will work things out for our good.*

# Black Man Eena De White House

What a ting a guan ma!
Jus look pon de wok a fate,
Me live fi see a black man
President of de United State.

When mi hear sey Obama win,
Mi feel like mi heart guan bus,
All a we should be so proud,
An it right we mek a fus?

An wen mi hear de speech mi dear,
Me dis a swell with pride
But de nicest ting in all a dis
Was when him family come by him side.

Mek mi tell yu bout dat Wednesday maaning,
When mi hear di news,
Mi jump outa bed like a mad woman
An fling awn mi clothes and shoes.

On di way to de paper shap
Me have big smile pon mi face,
Me sey 'good maaning' to everybody,
Mi feel like mi was ace.

Me walk eena mi staffroom,
An mi proudly announce
We have a new president,
A black man eena de White House!

Me walk eena mi classroom
Very proud a mi race,
Me call three pickney to di front
An mi tell dem face to face.

No matta how you look pon it
Everybody is a winna,
If yu black yu win.
If you white yu win.
An if yu brown yu win.
An if you mixed-heritage,
Well den, you REALLY win!

But den, eena the big scheme a tings
Does it really matta
Which shade a brown di man is?
When all a we a brada!

*'There is neither Jew nor Gentile, neither slave nor free, nor
is there male nor female, for you are all one in Christ Jesus.'
(Galatians 3:28)*

# Thank You Lord

Lord You knew the load I carried
Was too heavy to bear alone,

Lord You knew that  I was weary
And tired to the bone.

Lord You know the things I've been through,
The darkness of the past,

You know all about me
And that my sadness wouldn't last.

Lord I thank You that You knew me
When I was running wild.

Lord I thank You for the privilege
Of being called Your child,

Lord I thank You that You love me
And that for me You died;

I thank You that Your Holy Spirit
Will always, in me, abide.

Lord I thank You that the skies
Will one day be rolled back,

And for Your promise to us that
We will one day be where You are at.

*'Let not your hearts be troubled; you believe in God, believe
also in Me. In My Father's house are many mansions; if it were
not so, I would have told you. I go to prepare a place for you.
And if I go and prepare a place for you, I will come again and
receive you to Myself; that where I am there you may be also.'
(John 14:1-3).*

# That Sweet Spot

Father help me to find that sweet spot
Where You have created me to be,
Help me to find that sweet spot
Where Your love is all I see.


Father help me to find that sweet spot
Where my will is in line with Yours,
Help me to find that sweet spot
Where, like an eagle, I'll soar.


Father help me to find that sweet spot
Where my heart beats in anticipation,
Help me to find that sweet spot
Where I am one with Your creation.


Father help me to find that sweet spot
Where I am carried on the wings of Your grace,
Help me to find that sweet spot
Where I delight to run the race.

Father help me to find that sweet spot
Where I listen and obey,
Help me to find that sweet spot
Where I am walking in Your way.


*'He who has my commandments and keeps them it is he who
loves Me. And he who loves Me will be loved by My Father and
I will love him and manifest Myself to him.' (John 14:21)*

*This reference to 'sweet spot' comes from a chapter in a book
by Max Lucado, in which he suggests that our 'sweet spot' can
be recognised and measured by the pleasure we derive from
doing particular activities.*

# Just Enough Grace

Just enough grace for today Lord,

Just enough grace for the day.

Enough to get me out of bed,

Enough to get me clothed and fed.

Enough to smile at those I meet,

Enough to share, rather than to keep.

Enough to be reminded of the cross,

Enough to appreciate the cost!

Enough to demonstrate Your love,

Enough to thank You my Father above.

*'My grace is sufficient for you, for My strength is made perfect in  weakness.' (2 Corinthians 12:9)*

# Listening to the Father

I'm listening to You my Father,

I'm listening with all my heart.

I'm listening in the stillness,

I'm listening through the noise.

I'm listening in times of sadness

And in those times of gladness;

Keep me listening to You my Father,

Keep me listening with all my heart.

*'… Speak, for your servant is listening.'*
*(1 Samuel 3:10)*

*As Christians, we love to talk to God whether through prayer or singing but we sometimes forget to simply listen.*

# Speaking to the Father

What do you do when life's promises fall short,
When the pains are too real to share,
When fear destroys your inner peace
As hope crumbles to dust in your face,
And tomorrow is so far away?

What do you do as you wait by the phone,
Sitting in loneliness and despair,
When old guilt raises its ugly head, and
Uncertainties and doubts creep in,
With tomorrow so far away?

Speak to Elohim – Almighty God,
Sovereign Creator and Covenant Maker,
For He alone knows our heart.

Speak to Jehovah – the Revealer,
The unchanging One, your personal God,
For He alone knows our heart.

Speak to El Shaddai – All Sufficient God,
Who promises to supply all you need,
For He alone knows our heart.

Speak to Adonai – Master, Owner and Protector,
He wants to be Lord of your life,
For He alone knows our heart.

Speak to Jehovah Jireh – the Provider.
His plan of redemption was
Laid before the Earth's foundation,
For He alone knows our hearts.


*'For in Him we live and move and have our being.'*
*(Acts 17:28)*

*God reveals Himself to us through His names and there are*
*no circumstances  in our lives, in which we cannot call on God*
*through the use of a specific name.*

# My God is Real

Who says that my God isn't real
And doesn't answer prayers?
Who says that my God doesn't feel
Our joys, our pains, our fears?

Who says that my God doesn't hear
And doesn't hold our hands?
Who says that my God doesn't care
For you, for me, for all?

Who says that my God doesn't see
All that I'm going through?
Who says that my God cannot be
My love, my hope, my life?

Who says that my God cannot touch
My heart with tenderness?
Who says that my God is a crutch
For the weak, the meek and frail?

Who says that my God doesn't know
The me, deep down inside?
Who says that my God doesn't help me grow
More like Him, in every way?

I'll tell you this,
My God is real,
He sees and hears us all,
He touches hearts, He knows our frame.
Yes, the God I serve is real!


'For the message of the cross is foolishness to those who are
perishing, but to us who are being saved it is the power of
God.' (1 Corinthians 1:18)

# The Waiting Room

I sit waiting to be called,
Dreading every second,
Wanting to be called, but wanting to wait longer.

Can I deal with the wait
As fear dances all around?
Wanting to be called, but wanting to wait longer.

I survey the faces of others
In the waiting room,
Wanting to be called, but wanting to wait longer.

I could look down and read a mag
To while the time away,
Wanting to be called, but wanting to wait longer.

My name is called, it's my turn next!
What will they say to me?
Wanting to be called, but wanting to wait longer.

Is this a reflection of our Christian living
In the waiting room of life?
Wanting to be bold, but wanting to wait longer.

Do we allow fear to blight our lives
With self-doubt and reticence?
Wanting to step out in faith, but wanting to wait longer.

There is a need all around us
In the waiting room of life, so
With mercy, grace and  justice,
We step out in faith and love
To answer the commission call
From our heavenly Father above.

*'Go therefore and make disciples of all the nations, baptizing
them in the name of the Father and of the Son and of the Holy
Spirit.'  (Matthew 28:19)*

# Stepping Out

Lord, whenever fear and doubt creep into our minds,

Help us to step out in faith and leave them behind.

Lord help us to remember that You are our strength,

You are our strong tower,

You only are the life-giver.

You sent Your only son Jesus to lead us back to You,

Your Holy Spirit guides us, Your presence makes us new.

Lord, you've given us the armour; the helmet for our minds,

The breastplate which will guard our hearts, and the belt, Your truth to find.

The shield of faith to stand tall; the sword – Your holy Word,

And the good news of the Gospel, to share with the whole world.

*'For whom He foreknew, He also predestined to be conformed to the image of His Son, that He might be the firstborn among many brethren.' (Romans 8:29)*

# Surprise!

Won't we be surprised when we get to heaven
And see those we thought were lost,
Those we judged as 'less than',
Those we thought just couldn't be forgiven!

Won't we be surprised when we hear the welcome
Jesus saved just for them,
As He smiles, extends His hand and says
"Come in My daughter, come in My son!"

Won't we be surprised to see the other denominations,
Catholics, JWs, SDAs and Pentecostals,
The ones who were 'too quiet', 'too loud' or 'too pious',
With us at our final destination!

Won't we be surprised to see those of other faiths,
Who had in the past believed in other gods,
Having given their lives to the one true God,
Now standing with us, at the heavenly gates.

Remember the thief on the cross next to Christ
Who asked to be forgiven?
Christ forgave him all

And he was invited that day,
To be with the Father in heaven.

The truth is, one doesn't know how our God nurtures,
The way He touches the human heart,
And how with compassion, He draws us to Himself
Regardless of our past.


*I am always surprised at how quickly some Christians are to
condemn. I remember when Princess Diana died how some
were saying that she wouldn't go to heaven. Even though I did
not know the Lord back then I felt those Christians were making decisions that God alone makes. I am also troubled by the
way some Christian denominations feel they own the freehold
to heaven and only those of a particular denomination will be
there! Yes, the Bible tells us that there is only one way to the
Father and that is by acknowledging Jesus as Lord and Saviour,
but we simply do not know if in a person's last breath, they
have confessed Jesus as Lord. I am reminded of the verse in
Matthew 20:9-13 where all the workers regardless of how late
they started working received the same pay.*

*The point I would like to make here is that we shouldn't be
judgmental but we should keep praying for those we know and
love to come to faith in Jesus. Of course as Christians, we know
that the rewards for following Jesus begin here on earth as the
Holy Spirit pours His grace, mercy, love, forgiveness and peace
into our hearts. It is always wise therefore to accept Jesus as
Lord earlier rather than later, so that we can start enjoying
Kingdom living here on earth.*

# Whose Are You?

Do you see yourself as a victim,
Or victorious in the strife?
On this journey that we call life,
How do you see yourself?

Do you see yourself as a victim
When trials and pain overwhelm?
Or can you like Job, echo
God's sovereignty, again and again and again?

Do you see yourself as a victim,
Imprisoned by your past?
With guilt, shame and much regret
As the enemy whispers its lies.

Do you see yourself as a victim
As austerity tightens its grip?
Unemployment, homelessness on the rise
But no one to hear your silent cries.

Do you see yourself as a victim
Because of the colour of your skin?
Opportunities denied, and glass ceilings lowered
And threatening to box you in.

Do not let others define
The person you truly are,
Do not accept the labels
Or be forced to bear a scar.

Be the very best that you can be
In every area of your life,
Remembering in whose image you are made
And to whose calling you upwardly strive.

*'For I know the plans I have for you…' (Jeremiah 29:11)*

# Just Ask

Ask without doubting,
Ask always knowing
That our God will surely hear.
Ask with thanksgiving,
Ask the God of the living
And feel His presence near.

Ask without doubting,
Ask always knowing
That our God is a rewarder of those
Who seek Him sincerely,
And want to love dearly
Their friends, as well as their foes.

Ask without doubting,
Ask always knowing
God holds us in the palm of His hand.
He plans for us a future
Because love is His nature
And He asks us to take a stand.

A stand against injustice,
To listen and obey,
To act in compassion as we walk in His way.
To support the needy,
To protect the weak,
To be on Earth His hands and His feet.


*'Be anxious for nothing, but in everything by prayer and supplication, with thanksgiving, let your requests be made known to God.'     (Philippians 4:6)*

# Jesus Rap

Did you know that Jesus is the Messiah?
Who came from heaven so we could live better,
Unemployment, sickness, poor relationships –
I'm here to tell you that Jesus is higher.
Higher than you and higher than me
Is Jesus the Messiah who died on a tree.
Died in our place so we could be free,
Died to reconcile friends and family.
He died for you and He died for me.
Can't you see that Jesus is He?
Jesus is He! Yes Jesus is He!
Can't you see that Jesus is He?

*'For God so loved the world that He gave his only begotten
Son that whoever believes in Him will not perish but have
everlasting life.'*
*(John 3:16)*

*I love the rhythm, energy and engagement of the spoken word
and for me rapping is a great example of the power of the
spoken word.*

# Outstretched Hands

Your outstretched hands showed mercy,
Your lips forgiveness spoke,
Your readiness to die on a cross
Should in us true worship provoke.

Your long, lonely walk to Calvary,
Your stumbles, the jeers and the pain,
Your agony in those final hours
Should touch our hearts again and again.

Your love and determination
To put Yourself in our place,
Your promise to the thief while on that cross
Should inspire us to run the race.

Your death and resurrection,
Your glory with the Father above,
The promises in Your holy Word
Should prompt us to remain in Your love.

*'See, I have engraved you on the palms of my hands.'*
*(Isaiah 49:16)*

# Every Step

Each step to the cross forgiveness brought,

Each step You took for us.

Mercy freely given and grace poured out

Because of Your great love.

You stumbled and fell, yet carried on,

You hurt, You bled, yet carried on;

Sent from heaven, God's only Son,

To die for me, to die for all.

Committed no sin yet paid the price

So we can live in love and hope.

Each step You took it was for us,

Steps of sadness, pain and sorrow,

Steps for the joy yet to come.

Thank You Lord for every step.

Thank You for Your great love.

*'Greater love has no one than this, than to lay down one's life for his friends.' (John 15:13)*

# The Pentecost Power

The Pentecost power is available today,
Our Heavenly Father wants to have His way,
He's promised a fresh outpouring on our nations,
On men and women, across the generations.

The Pentecost power is available to us
And needs to be accessed as a must!
So we stand on His word
And pray for that stirring to happen,
As it did at the waters, when healing was given.

The Pentecost power wasn't a one-off,
We needn't be fearful when others scoff,
They did that to the disciples
On that day in Jerusalem,
When they laughed and mocked again and again.

The Pentecost power is a promise to the Church,
So we don't stand around as though left in the lurch,
Through the power of the Spirit we can change
situations,
Let's position ourselves to be that beacon to the nations.

The Pentecost power can be a reality in our life,
As we walk by faith and not by sight,
We can reach a hungry world yearning for God's truth
To make them whole again, and so bear fruit.

The Pentecost power, O what joy!
That through Jesus' sacrifice sin was destroyed!
Let's stand up and celebrate God's victory at the cross,
It is finished! It is finished!
Sin and death have lost.


*'See, I am doing a new thing! Now it springs up; do you not perceive it? I am making a way in the wilderness and streams in the wastelands.' (Isaiah 43:19)*

# The Enemy Within

The enemy isn't racism,
Insidious and ugly from the start;
The real enemy lies closer
And it's about time we start to talk.

The real enemy is oppression,
The real enemy is fear,
The real enemy is injustice,
The real enemy is ever so near!

So when we look at our TV screens
And see yet another case
Of people dying needlessly
Regardless of their race.

We need to ask the question,
Uncomfortable though it may be,
What on earth has gone wrong
With humanity?

Why should the poor be so oppressed
When there's enough to go around?
Why so many living on the streets?
Why so many dispossessed?

Why is fear the covering
For so many decent folk?
The despair etched on their faces
Makes us want to choke!

Why does injustice ominously seep into
Every aspect of our life?
In fact, it is so tangible
You could cut it with a knife!

We need to see the enemy
With all its different spikes
And realize that racism
Is just one type of vice.

So let us take a closer look
At what is really happening here,
We see a world hell-bent on greed,
When there's more than enough to share.

*'He has shown you, O man, what is good, and what does the Lord require of you but to do justly, to love mercy and to walk humbly with your God. ' (Micah 6:8)*

*'But let justice roll down like waters, and righteousness like an ever-flowing stream. ' (Amos 5:24)*

# Trust and Faith

Trust and faith are two little words,
Easy to say, but hard to obey;
When the trials of this world knock us about
And trust and faith are replaced by doubt,

The Father says:

'Trust Me,
I've given you the faith,
Though small as a mustard seed
Amongst weeds of doubt,
It will grow like an oak tree, degree by degree.'

So

Abandon yourself to the Father's care,
Lean on Him, take His hand, He'll get you there.
The road of life's journey can sometimes be tough
But Jesus softly whispers,

'I AM  ENOUGH.'

*'Take My yoke upon you and learn from Me, for I am gentle
and in humble in heart, and you will find rest for your souls.'
(Matthew 11:29)*

# More of You Lord

I just want to walk with You,
I just want to talk with You,
I just want to hold Your hand
And take a stand for You.
I just want to seek Your face
And to stand in Your grace,
I just want more of You.

Jesus,
I just want to welcome You,
I just want to worship You,
I just want to tell You
That You are my all-in-all;
I just want more of  You.

Jesus,
I just want more of You.

*'Taste and see that the Lord is good.'  (Psalm 34:8)*

# Why? Why? Why?

Ripped from the arms of Mama Africa

For the journey across a sea of despair,

Families separated, people loaded onto ships.

Take time to listen, and you will hear

Their plaintive cries of

Why? Why? Why?

Chained together in an ocean of blackness,

Enduring suffering and abuses of all kinds,

Thrown alive into the jaws of the hungry Atlantic.

Take time to stop, and look to see

The agony on their faces.

Why? Why? Why?

Arriving in the Americas and the Caribbean,

Being sold as chattels, cargo and goods,

Forbidden to speak their language, to dance, or to sing,

Take time to touch, you will feel

The scars inside and out.

Why? Why? Why?

Given new 'Christian' names and branded.

Fathers beaten in front of children,

Females raped and children dragged away.

Take time to smell the pungent, putrid odour of hate,

Why? Why? Why?

And they say we are all made in God's image,

Why then all this savagery?

Why do you wish evil against me?

You enslaved me!

Humiliated me!

Tortured me!

Stole from me!

Sneered at me!

Lied about me!

Killed me!

But here I am, tall and proud,

I'm the one who stands out in the crowd,

See, God has turned it around for my good!

I will not be defined by my past,

Your opinion of me will not last.

I choose to live in the present today,

You will no longer have your way,

I choose to hold my head up high…

Because I choose…to forgive.


*'Forgive us today our sins, for we also forgive everyone who sins against us.' (Luke 11:4)*

*'We are hard pressed on every side, yet not crushed; we are perplexed, but not in despair; persecuted, but not forsaken, struck down but not destroyed.' (2 Corinthians 4:8-9)*

# The Lesson

There's a lesson in every heartache
And a lesson in every fear,
There's a lesson in every challenge
To remind us that God is near.

There's a lesson in every pain we feel,
And in every circumstance,
Nature flaunts that lesson daily,
Reminding us that God is real.

Yes, there's a lesson on the mountain top
And in the valleys too,
There's a lesson in the lesson,
Confirming to us that God is true.

*'I will lift up my eyes to the hills, from whence comes my help?
My help comes from the Lord, who made heaven and earth.'
(Psalm 121:1-2)*

# Hope

Today I looked in the mirror
And there looking back at me
Was someone I almost failed to recognise,
It had been such a long time you see.

There looking back at me with wisdom,
Strength, understanding and grace
Was Hope;
A friend I thought I'd lost,
How it touched my heart to see her face.

Hope gave me the strength to carry on
When the world was bleak and grey,
Hope has never disappointed me
And Hope always leads the way.

Hope provided friendship and comfort
And was my companion day after day,
Hope springs eternal
When we follow the Saviour's way.

Today I looked in the mirror,
And there looking back at me
With kindness and understanding,
With certainty and love,
With determination and grace,
Was Hope;
It was so good to see her face.


*'May the God of hope fill you with all joy and peace in
believing, that you may abound in hope by the power of the
Holy Spirit.' (Romans 15:13)*

# The Power of Prayer

What if prayer was the cord to turn a famine into a
feast?
What if prayer was the cord to save a loved one's life?
What if prayer was the cord to end all strife?
The catalyst to ignite that latent flame into an inferno of
hope and peace.
What if prayer was that cord?
The cord we could weave into life's situations,
A cord so strong, it defies gravitation
But reaches to the heavens,
And transforms a nation.
What if prayer was that cord?
Sometimes we find ourselves busy,
Far too busy to pray
But, what if…
What if prayer released God's glory
To experience healings,
To fan the flame of love and understanding?
What if prayer is the testimony our world needs?
What if?
What if?
What if?
Would you pray
More regularly?

Fervently?
Faithfully?
Humbly?
Expectantly?
Excitedly?
But prayer is that cord,
The cord that
Brings us into the Father's presence,
The cord that offers hope,
The cord that fills us with awe
And changes us inside out.
Yes! Prayer is that cord!

'…one of his disciples said to him, "Lord, teach us to pray." '
(Luke 11:1)

# We Must Breathe

The slave-catchers are after me,

I can't breathe!

I'm thrown into the waiting cells of Elmina Castle,

We can't breathe!

Chained together in the hold of the ship,

We can't breathe!

Disease and illness rife,

We can't breathe!

Toiling on the plantations,

Their whips scar us,

We can't breathe!

In the Motherland

Racism wants to choke us,

Institutions want to destroy us,

Hatred wants to exterminate us!


We           can't           breathe!


But, breathe we must.

We breathe so that the songs of the slaves will not be forgotten;

Twelve million enslaved over 400 years.

We breathe so that our ancestors' lives will not have been in vain,

Nanny of the Maroons, Fredrick Douglas, Equano and more.

We breathe so that those giants on whose shoulders we stand

Will remain a strong monument for future generations.

And with every breath, we rise from the agony of the past,

With every breath, we give hope to our children,

With every breath we nurture their confidence,

And as we exhale, we do so in the knowledge that
together we are stronger

And that love will always win.

So we say,

Breathe freely those yet to be born,

Breathe freely our future,

Breathe freely my people,

Breathe freely.


*'And the Lord God formed man of the dust of the ground, and
breathed into his nostrils the breath of life; and man became a
living being.' (Genesis 2:7)*

*'Then the Lord said to Cain, "Where is Abel your brother?" He
said, " I do not know, Am I my brother's keeper?"'
(Genesis 4:9)*

*Throughout history people have used the murder of others as
a sport. Crowds flocked to the Colosseum in Rome to watch
Christians and others being killed. Christian martyrs were
burnt at the stake, while others looked on. 'Witches' were also
burnt while 'the religious Christian' mob looked on cheering.
Lynching was a popular sport in the U.S. and parents would
take young children to watch. But to see on our T.V. screens in
2020 such a  brutal murder and to hear the dying words as life
ebbed away was heart-wrenching.*

*This poem is a direct response to the murder of Mr. George
Floyd. A Christian friend stressed that we shouldn't condemn
the person, but condemn instead the spirit of evil in the person.*

# Who do you say I am?

When you look at me who do you see?

Nurse?
Cleaner?
Transport worker?
Woman?
Mother?
Teacher?
Doctor?
Lawyer?
Christian?
Muslim?
A Person?
Or do you just see BLACK?

When I look at me
I see years of struggle,
I see an inner strength that has defied all the odds.
I see the hope of my ancestors,
I see the yearning of generations past and those yet to come.
And no, I'm not colour-blind,
So I too see me, BLACK.

Strange isn't it?
You might say we see the same thing
But our perspectives are so very different.
You see me through the lens of bigotry,
I see me because of your bigotry.

So can we talk about it?
This hate you have for me,
When did it first rear its ugly head?
And why, O why, does it want me dead?


*'The music of the piano is made universal by the use of two
sets of keys: ebony and ivory.'*  pb

*'Only in the darkness can we see the stars.'*
Martin Luther King (Jr)

# Renew my Mind

Renew my mind, Lord, renew my mind.
Renew my mind, Lord, renew my mind.
Sometimes we feel lost, worthless and unsure,
Sinking in self-pity and paralysed by fear –
Am I good enough?
Will I make the cut?
Remember, remember that God is near.
Renew my mind, Lord, renew my mind.
Renew my mind, Lord, renew my mind.


Now listen to this –
You're in the classroom,
Someone cuts you down
With unkind words that bring on a frown.
You feel you've been 'dissed',
You're burning inside,
But remember, remember that God is near.
Renew my mind, Lord, renew my mind.
Renew my mind, Lord, renew my mind.

Hear this –
You're driving in the car, already late,
Someone cuts in on you.
You scream 'Can't you wait?'
Anger starts to boil
And your peace is gone,
But remember, remember that God is near.
Renew my mind, Lord, renew my mind.
Renew my mind, Lord, renew my mind.

You work for ten years giving all you've got,
Someone new comes in and they're where it's at;
The years of slogging and those late nights –
Was it all worth it? What do I do now?
Just remember, remember that God is near.
Renew my mind, Lord, renew my mind.
Renew my mind, Lord, renew my mind.

With a mind renewed we see things differently,
With a mind renewed we seek God actively,
With a mind renewed we let go of the past,
With a mind renewed we know evil won't last.
So renew my mind, Lord, renew my mind.
Renew my mind, Lord, renew my mind.

*'Do not conform to the pattern of this world, but be trans-
formed by the renewing of your mind. Then you will be able to
test and approve what God's will is…'   (Romans 12:2)*

*There is a rhythm to this poem which makes it well suited to be
delivered powerfully as a rap.*

# Choices

You have a choice my sister,

You have a choice today.

Will you follow the world of self

Or walk the Saviour's way?

You have a choice my brother,

As you awaken from a night of rest.

The choice to join in with the crowd,

Or give to God your best.

You have a choice my neighbour,

As you strive for worldly gain.

The choice to work at what really counts

And trust in Jesus' name.

You have a choice my colleague,

As you rush around getting diary dates.

The choice to stop awhile and listen

And to exercise some faith.


You have a choice today my friend,

A choice that's yours alone:

To serve a living, loving God,

Or to face life spiritually alone.


*'If you knew the gift of God and who it is that asks you for a
drink, you would have asked him and he would have given
you living water.' (John 4:10)*

# The Counsellor

Is it any wonder that Jesus Christ our Lord
Has been a Mighty Counsellor from the days of old?
He counselled Adam in the beginning
To take care of His garden home,
To obey His voice and walk with Him,
And live forevermore.

He counselled Abram in Haran
To trust in Him alone,
To leave his home and walk by faith
Into the unknown.

He counselled Noah to build a boat,
His neighbours mocked and jeered.
Noah listened to God's counsel
And his family were saved.

He counselled Joseph in his prison cell
And he interpreted Pharoah's dreams.
Storehouses were built, lives were saved
Because of Joseph's schemes.

He counselled Moses on the journey
Into the Promised Land.
From tribulations they were saved
By God's almighty hand.

And what of Joshua, the judges and kings?
What of the prophets, and Paul?
From Genesis to Revelation you will find
That, yes, our Great God counselled them all.

The Spirit continues His counsel
In all our lives today.
And all He gently asks is that
We listen and obey.


*'I will instruct you and teach you in the way you should go; I will guide you with My eye.' (Psalm 32:8)*

*'…His name shall be called Wonderful, Counsellor, Mighty God, Everlasting Father, Prince of Peace.' (Isaiah 9:6)*

# The Gentiles Bless Zion

Arise and shine for your light has come

And the glory of the Lord is risen on you.

For behold

The darkness shall cover the earth,

The deep, deep darkness of the people.

But the Lord will arise over you,

Yes, the Lord will arise over you.

And His glory will be seen on you,

Yes, His glory will be seen on you.

So arise, shine for your light has come

And the glory of the Lord is risen on you,

Yes, arise, shine for your light has come

And the glory of the Lord is risen on you.

The Gentiles shall come to your light,

And kings to the brightness of your rising.

Your sons shall come from afar,

And your daughters shall be nursed at your side.

So, arise, shine for your light has come

And the glory of the Lord has risen on you.

Yes, arise, shine for your light has come

And the glory of the Lord is on you.

*(Isaiah 60)*

*As I was reading one morning, I found myself bopping to an internal rhythm.  As I explored that rhythm further it seemed to naturally lend itself to a rap so I played around with the words and came up with this.*

# The Deafening Silence

The voice of God thundered
Across timeless space,
Like a gushing ocean
In an empty place.

His Word pierced the silence
And the darkness rolled back,
As out of the void
The Light attacked.

The stars sang out in worship
As they were hurled into the void,
The moon and sun echoed
In praise to Jehovah God.

God continued His creation
By shaping the Earth;
Mountains, valleys and oceans
Were all being birthed.

God loved what He'd made
But He desired so much more,
A people of worship
Was what He had in store.

From out of the clay
God shaped the first man.
Then breathed life-giving power
And gave him control of the land.


Yes, all of creation for man to control,
To be good stewards of His benevolent store.


But,


Greed led to wars
To famine,
Flooding,
And fires,
With people displaced
And in fear of their lives.


The voice of God thunders
Across planet earth;
Is anyone listening
As destruction is being birthed?


The voice of God whispers
In silent pain.
The voice of God whispers
Again and again.


*Perhaps my all-time favourite poem was written by the black
American James Weldon Johnson in the 1930s, and entitled
'The Creation.' It is a powerful representation of the Genesis*

*creation story, but it is also much more than that. It allows you to imagine our God in His majesty and power, standing in the vast nothingness of space, speaking prophetically and life bubbling up all around Him. The tear-jerking moment is when God in all His glory stoops down to create man – majesty and meekness in week one of creation!*

*I hope that this poem presents an image almost as powerful as that presented by James Weldon Johnson. The last three stanzas look at the consequences of man's indifference to God's creation and remind us that God is still speaking to us today.*

# I Shout Because You're God

I shout because I'm victorious,
I shout because I'm saved.
I shout because You love me,
I shout because You gave.

Jesus You took the fall,
Jesus You paid it all,
Jesus my life You saved,
Jesus new life You gave.

Jesus my life You saved,
Jesus the price You paid.
Jesus to You I bring
My worship, my everything.

I shout because You gave:
Your life,
Your all,
Your grace,
Your love.
I shout because You ARE God!

*'Make a joyful shout to the Lord, all you lands! Serve the Lord
with gladness; come before His presence with singing.'
(Psalm 100:1-2)*

# Hallelujah, Our God Reigns

Father we thank You that You reign on high.
You reign when it's sunny,
You reign when it rains,
You reign in our joys,
And You reign in our pains.

You reign in righteousness
For You are a Holy God.
You reign in peace
For You are Shalom.

You are the banner we hold up high.
You are forever faithful
For You cannot lie.
You are our healer, provider and guide,
Father You reign on high.

You are Elohim, creator of life.
You are El Elyon, the Most High God,
You are El Shaddai our All Sufficient One,
Father You reign on high.

You are Jehovah Gmolah, our recompense,
For You promise to repay and to compensate.

You are Jehovah Makkeh who breaks to make new,
You are Jehovah M'Kaddesh who sanctifies all,
Father You reign on high.

You are Jehovah Shammah
For You are there,
Your Spirit within us,
Your presence around us,
Your joy is our strength,
Your living Word our hope.
Hallelujah Father,
Please reign in our lives.

*'I am the Alpha and the Omega, the Beginning and the End,
says the Lord, who is and who was and who is to come, the
Almighty.'
(Revelation 1:8)*

# Who are we Lord?

Who are we Lord?
But runaway children,
Yet You promise never to leave us alone.
Who are we Lord?
But a people puffed up with self-pride,
Yet You call us the apple of Your eye.

Who are we Lord?
But a people battered by the storms of life,
Yet You rejoice over us with singing.
Who are we Lord?
But those dressed in filthy rags,
Yet You hold us in the palm of Your hand.

Who are we Lord?
But sin-drenched mortals,
Yet every hair on our head is numbered by You.
Who are we Lord?
But a people lamenting,
Yet You have promised us Your peace.

Who are we Lord?
But repentant sinners,
Transformed by Your mercy and grace.

Thank you Lord that we are children of the King,
Thank you Lord so to You we sing,
Thank you Lord for the freedom You give,
Thank you Lord that in You we live!


*'He lifted me out of the slimy pit, out of the mud and mire; he
set my feet on a rock and gave me a firm place to stand. He
put a new song in my mouth, a hymn of praise to our God.
Many will see and fear the Lord and put their trust in him.'
(Psalm 40:2-3)*

# When Prayer is More Than Just Words

When prayer becomes more than just words
Something changes.
A drum roll of the heart,
The spirit is engaged,
The soul is excited,
God responds,
Miracles happen.

You see,
When prayer becomes more than just words
There is a shift in the spiritual realm,
Which creates an alignment between heaven and earth
And allows the spirit within us
To tap into
The supernatural power of God.

You see,
When prayer becomes more than just words
Our eyes are opened,
Our hearts are quickened
Our souls hunger and thirst
Our spirits respond,
And God is glorified.

You see,
When prayer becomes more than just words
We move to a different plane,
It's not about us, but the power of God in us,
Mountains become mounds,
Problems become challenges,
The impossible becomes possible,
When prayers becomes more than just words.

You see,
Prayer is not an Aladdin's lamp
To pick up in desperation,
Prayer is not a talisman or a lucky charm.
Prayer is more than scripted words we read and say
'Amen'
Prayer is not a last resort,
It is a way of living.

You see,
Prayer is organic with a life force of its own,
Prayer is powerful, more powerful than is known,
Prayer brings us together as one
And shakes principalities.

The impossible becomes possible
When prayer becomes more than just words.

*'Confess your trespasses to one another, and pray for one another, that you may be healed. The effective, fervent prayer of a righteous man avails much.'*
*(James 5:16)*

# PART TWO

# A personal interpretation of how God reveals Himself in the 23rd Psalm

As a child and later as a young adult, I struggled to understand the peace, comfort and contentment that this Psalm offered. Funerals had left me associating this Psalm always with death, and so it was never one of my 'go to' Psalms even as a young Christian.

As my faith-walk matured, and the uneasiness around death and dying were erased, I began to appreciate the beauty, compassion, restoration and love embedded in this Psalm.

Throughout scripture, God has revealed Himself to His people in different ways. It is easy to see God as the Good Shepherd – Jehovah Rohi – in the 23rd Psalm, but I also believe that there are many other names through which God reveals Himself in this Psalm.

I hope that this reflection will enable the reader to come to a deeper spiritual interpretation of this Psalm for their lives.

**'The Lord is my Shepherd, I shall not be in want.'**
This verse for me sums up the whole of Psalm 23. When we make the Lord our Shepherd we can never be in want. We see Jehovah Rohi here, but we also see El Shaddai – God who is all sufficient – our God who is more than enough. Let's spend some time thinking about the qualities of a shepherd first.

A shepherd leads his flock and as he does so, he is acutely aware of their needs and the dangers around. The shepherd's first concern is for the wellbeing of his flock, and so the flock will never be in want because the shepherd has taken care of their wants by paying attention to their needs.

Jesus our Shepherd has promised to supply our every need according to His riches in Glory. El Shaddai owns the cattle on a thousand hills; the Earth is the Lord's and everything in it, so it should not come as a surprise to us, that God is always providing. He knows what we need before we ask Him. With such a shepherd, how can we ever be in want?

**Prayer:** *Thank You Saviour and Shepherd that You promise to supply my every need. Thank You that I can never be in want.*

**'He makes me to lie down in green pastures.'**
The Shepherd leads us and never leaves us. He brings us into restful places and situations. He says to us, "Chill, relax, enjoy my creation. Take as long as you need, there is so much here for your mind, body and spirit. Everything

you need is here, take time out from the busyness of life, 'Be still and know that I am God.' I want to meet with you, to refresh you, to give you peace. Rest awhile my child. I love you, please take time out." Here we catch a glimpse of Elohim, our God who 'In the beginning, created the heavens and the earth.' Our God who rested on the seventh day as an example to us.

Our Shepherd, Saviour, our Elohim, places green pastures in all our lives. He wants to meet with us and He wants us to enjoy His green pastures. He wants us to understand that His provision for us will be different from His provision for our closest friend. He doesn't want us to worry about what He has provided for others. His word tells us that He knows what we need before we even ask. He doesn't want envy and jealousy to be a part of our lives. He wants us to simply enjoy His provisions as He takes us to that holy place of peace, love and contentment where all we need to do is receive. What green pastures has the Lord led you to, so that you can enjoy His fullness and the beauty of His creation?

**Prayer:** *Heavenly Father, Thank You for all your provisions. Thank You for the opportunities to listen to music, read books, have conversations with others and to be with family and friends. Thank You for the green pastures of peace, the sense of Your presence and the awesomeness of Your majesty that prayer provides.*

## 'He leads me beside the quiet waters.'

How lovely to have still waters in green pastures. After we have rested from the cares of the world, enjoying the green pastures, the relaxation is extended and enhanced by the Shepherd leading us beside the still waters. We can simply look into the clear cool water and have our relaxed selves look back at us. Picture the view! A green landscape with pools of still water for a time of quiet refreshment. Such peace. It is here we meet and enjoy the presence of Jehovah Shalom.

The Lord leads us beside the still waters, He doesn't lead us into the still waters. Why not? Well the choice is ours. We can paddle or float or simply dangle our feet in the water. It is generally not dangerous because there is very little current – just enough for us to appreciate the movement. The water is there to refresh us, it's there to be used, so how we make use of the water is very much up to us. I sometimes listen to the sound of water as I drift off to sleep, it always fills me with peace. Do we need to have a refreshing soak, or do we just need to listen and look, perhaps at the water birds making mesmerising ripples as they too refresh themselves?

Jesus our Shepherd, leads us to safe pastures with refreshing still waters, where He is always there to protect us from life's predators. He knows that some seemingly still waters can be dangerous so He keeps close to us at all times. If a sheep should fall into water, their wool could drag them down as it becomes saturated, and this could lead to drowning. The Shepherd is therefore always on hand to rescue. Sometimes we find ourselves in situations which could overwhelm us, but as we follow Jesus' leading and trust His mercy, we begin to realise what a wonderful Shepherd He is to us. After all, He is the Good Shepherd!

As you are being led beside still waters today, why don't you simply enjoy His company, His provision, and His peace as you 'taste and see that the Lord is good'?

**Prayer:** *Good Shepherd, thank You for providing still waters for us to enjoy. Thank You for the views. Thank You that You are Jehovah Shalom – our perfect peace. Thank You for the choices You give us. Help us to listen to Your advice and make us more aware of the need to relax and enjoy the peace and beauty of Your creation.*

### 'He restores my soul.'

Only by the still waters of life can our souls be restored. Over the days, weeks, months and years our souls become weary and sometimes broken. We need to linger for as long as it takes to be restored. As we wait for the restoration of our souls, in the presence of the great healer Jehovah Rophe, there is healing for body, mind and spirit. What a care-giving Shepherd we have!

Restoration takes time. God breathed into Adam the breath of life and he became a living soul. Our souls work in harmony with the rest of our bodies and when disharmony occurs it can cause all kinds of illness. We need to ensure that our souls are always in a state of restoration. We need to linger by the 'still waters', spending quality time with our Shepherd, reading His living Word, worshipping and praying. We need to make time.

Restoration is an attitude. We must acknowledge that we are not super-human and need to take time out for refreshment. We must stop wallowing in fear, doubt and self-pity and climb up out of the paralysing depths of negative thoughts. It is by the still waters that we renew our minds.

The Shepherd uses us to restore others and uses others to bring about restoration in us. One of the greatest privileges of teaching is to simply watch or listen to children at play. The noise, shrills of excitement and laughter is like medicine. Godly friends, colleagues, older mentors, medics and pastors are just some of the people the Shepherd places on our paths on the way to restoration. Rest awhile my child, 'I will restore the years the locusts have eaten.'

**Prayer:** *Gracious loving Father, I am so sorry for going my way for so long, for not spending time in the green pastures of Your Word and Your world, for not following You to the still waters of life and allowing You to restore my soul. Lord whatever it takes I just want to follow You, to rest and enjoy You, to learn from You and to keep being restored by You.*

## 'He guides me in the paths of righteousness for his name's sake.'

Why does the Good Shepherd lead us in the paths of righteousness? The next phrase provides us with the answer – 'For His name's sake.' The Shepherd is holy, just, loving, faithful, merciful and righteous therefore He cannot deny Himself. Since He cannot deny Himself, it follows therefore that the only paths He can lead us along are right paths.

We are covered in His righteousness as we are being led. He has rescued us, redeemed us and justified us by His righteousness. He wants us to be holy because He is holy, and He wants us to respect and honour His name. As Paul tells us, we have no righteousness of our own, but as we choose to stay close to the Shepherd on our journey of life, we become more and more like Him as we walk in His righteousness.

Oh the blessing to be covered in the righteousness of Christ! When we walk in righteousness we are walking with Jehovah Tsidkenu – Jehovah our Righteousness – a name of God first revealed in Jeremiah chapter 23.

**Prayer:** *Good Shepherd – Jehovah Tsidkenu – I thank You that You are my leader and I am made right in You. Thank You that You know all the paths because You have walked them when You were here on Earth. Thank You Father that You clothe me in the righteousness of Your Son. Thank You for redeeming me at Calvary. Lord I pray that I will follow Your leading and walk with You along right paths. May I never dishonour Your holy name.*

**'Even though I walk through the valley of the shadow of death, I will fear no evil, for You are with me.'**
Oh the darkness of those days! Oh the despair, the loss of energy, the worry. How we long to speak God's truth into our lives, but we lack the energy and sometimes the conviction. All we can do in those 'valley seasons' is to trust, trust, trust, because He who promised is faithful.

At these times the Shepherd speaks softly and gently to us, "Be not afraid, I am with you." At these times the Shepherd lifts us on His strong shoulders and carries us through the valley before placing us on solid ground. What a Shepherd! Always close by to recognise when we need to feel His presence even closer. The Shepherd doesn't give us more than He knows our frail bodies can handle and reminds us that if we trust, all things WILL work out for His glory and our good in the end. We do not need to fear evil or evil-doers because the presence of Jehovah Rohi is always with us. And those who believe and call on the name of Jesus, through the power of His Holy Spirit, will be answered. The living Word in us, brings comfort as it opens us up to the work of the Holy Spirit in our lives. Praise is good medicine during these valley seasons, but our Shepherd knows and understands that at these times we may choose to praise with our hearts rather than our lips.

The years 2020 to 2022 were challenging for all of us in one way or another, and some of us indeed walked through the valley of the shadow of death. The greatest sadness was that we were, in most cases, simply not able to attend funerals or indeed to express our feelings by just reaching out with a hug.

God revealed Himself to Ezekiel as Jehovah Shammah which means 'Jehovah is there.' Jesus our Shepherd, Saviour and Friend walks with us in the valley of the shadow of death. Yes, He is right there alongside us, reminding us not to be afraid. Remember, His Word tells us that in our weakness, He is made strong.

**Prayer:** *Loving Shepherd, Jehovah Shammah, thank You for being my guide, Saviour and friend. Thank You for Your promise to be always with me especially in those lonely valley experiences when situations can become overwhelming. Thank You that my name is carved in the palm of Your hands. Help me to remember that when I am overwhelmed, the power of El Shaddai overshadows me, and that You are there in my circumstances.*

### 'Your rod and Your staff, they comfort me.'

Here we meet Jehovah Makkeh – the Lord our Smiter – who wants to shape, perfect and mould us so that we can become the people He has called us to be. We also meet Jehovah M'Kaddesh, the God who sanctifies. We are set apart to live holy lives dedicated to God. This is our reasonable service as God's workmanship.

God's Word is the rod and staff of life supporting us. The staff was a means of support for shepherds in biblical times and for us today it symbolises the rest we find in Jesus when we return to the fold. In biblical times a shepherd would use the crooked end of his staff to pull a sheep out of a dangerous situation and in a similar way God promises to protect us, and His Holy Spirit convicts us when we are tempted to go astray.

The rod was used by shepherds to fight off attacks from wild animals that would prey on the sheep, and in this way we see the rod of God as an instrument of protection. It was used by Moses to strike the rock providing water for the children of Israel to drink, therefore protecting them by providing for their health needs.

Rather than being fearful of the rod and staff, let us welcome the comfort they bring, knowing that in the hand of the Shepherd, the staff convicts our spirits when we wander away from God, and the rod is a force of protection around us. In the New Testament, Paul urges Timothy to use the word to correct, rebuke and encourage. Today, we have that same living Word, the rod and staff.

**Prayer:** *Heavenly Father, I thank You that You are ever present with us. Thank You Jehovah Makkeh for Your Holy Spirit at work in our lives moulding and shaping us. Thank You Jehovah M'Kaddesh that You sanctify us as You build us up into Your holy temple. Father thank You for Your rod and staff that support, guide and protect us.*

**'You prepare a table before me in the presence of my enemies.'**

After the provision, comfort, restoration and the walk through that valley of shadow, comes the provision from the Lord's table. He invites us to eat and replenish our heart, mind, body and spirit. He invites us to enjoy Him and the goodness, holiness and righteousness He offers. We sit at table with Jehovah Jireh our provider. We sit at table with Jehovah Gmolah – the Lord of recompense – who sees what we have gone through and promises to restore. This is the same God who has promised to 'restore the years the locusts have eaten.' We are reminded of Elijah, running scared, sitting under a tree and praying for death. The Lord, our good Shepherd, sends an angel to provide him with food and drink.

As we enjoy the blessings that the Lord has lavished on us, there will be others looking on. We may think we have no enemies because we are fair minded, easy going and understanding. Maybe we should re-think that premise and ask the Lord to open our eyes and give us discerning spirits to those around us, as we are warned in Proverbs about those, whose 'words are softer than oil, yet they are drawn swords.'

As your circumstances change, some may not like to see you being blessed, as it is said that 'misery loves company.' However, as every Christian knows, when our ways are pleasing to God our enemies will live at peace with us. If God is for us, who would indeed dare to be against us?

As the Lord our Shepherd leads us towards the table He has prepared for us He whispers, my child I have prepared a feast for you. 'Weeping may endure for a night but joy comes in the morning.' (Psalm 30:5)

**Prayer:** *Kind and gracious Heavenly Father, thank You for taking me into today. Without You where would I be? Thank You for those words which bring light, comfort and assurance during those desperate times. Thank You for carrying me when it got too rough for me. Thank You for the special table You have prepared for me, a table where those who call on Your name are always made welcome. Open my eyes and give me discernment to recognise those people, ideas and thoughts that need to be left behind as You renew my mind to the truth of Your Word. Show me how to enjoy the milli-seconds of life at Your table. May I indeed taste and see that You are good.*

### 'You anoint my head with oil; my cup runs over.'

Our loving Shepherd who instructs, guides, protects, carries, encourages, provides feast times for us, and now anoints us with the oil of gladness! He tells us that we are precious in His sight, our tears are in a bottle, He says we are the apple of His eye and He has our names carved in the palm of His hands. He invites us to keep drinking at His fountain of life. The joy of the Lord is indeed our strength! This is El Elyon, the Most High God.

In the Bible, oil was used for anointing priests and for the articles in the tabernacle; later on it was used to anoint kings. When anointed they were set apart as a holy vessel. When the Lord anoints us, He is setting us apart and inviting us to live holy lives to Him. This overflow of blessings is a sign of the goodness of God in our lives.

When we come through challenges we must be intentional in our recognition and praise-giving to a God who fills and refills us with blessings, so much that we overflow. Our cup of praise to the Lord should overflow in heart-felt thanks and praise for taking us through the difficult and the good times, for being our Father and most importantly, for being who He is – the Most High God.

**Prayer:** *Heavenly Father, Thank You for anointing me with Your oil of healing, gladness and peace. Thank You for rest. Thank You for Your love. May my cup of gratitude always overflow in praise of who You are, El Elyon, the Most High God.*

### 'Surely goodness and mercy shall follow me all the days of my life.'

When the Shepherd anoints us, we can be sure that His cup of goodness and love will overflow and He will be a good companion to us all the days of our lives.

With Jehovah Nissi as our banner, goodness and mercy follow closely behind. God is faithful to us. The plans He has for us are plans to prosper. God is love and He wants to bless us with His generosity. He wants His blanket of love to be around us always. As we bask in the goodness and mercy of our Shepherd we are constantly being reminded of His faithfulness, forgiveness and sacrifice – the price He paid for the relationship we enjoy with the Father. How should we then respond to the Lord's goodness and mercy?

Enjoy it – take time to reflect on the pattern of God's goodness in our individual lives and simply thank Him as we enjoy His provision.

Use it to bless others – the Lord blesses us so that we can bless others. We need to share our blessings with others by giving, encouraging, supporting and praying for others so that our lives reflect His glory.

**Prayer:** *I thank You for these words of comfort. I thank You that Your promises are true. Thank You that Your goodness and mercy follow me daily. Thank You that as Your children, we carry Your essence – a symbol of Your presence – around with us. Father, there are times when I doubt, please forgive me; there are times when I'm afraid, please forgive me; there are times when I find it difficult to read Your word, please forgive me. Father help me to determine to live in Your grace, Your goodness and Your mercy all the days of my life. Help me to always hold Your banner high, to reach out and share with others the love, mercy and compassion of the Shepherd, our Risen Lord.*

### 'And I will dwell in the house of the Lord forever.'

The Shepherd wants us to abide in His presence. If we truly want to dwell in the house of the Lord and enjoy the blessing that the presence of Adonai offers, we need to be obedient to His Word. Our lives need to reflect His peace, love, mercy and compassion. As we draw near to the Shepherd, we are filled so we can give out to others and be filled again. Adonai is Lord of our lives, He is our Master, we reverence Him because He is God and we serve Him by serving others.

Living in the house of the Lord begins here on earth, wherever we find ourselves. Remember the prayer Jesus taught His disciples, 'Thy kingdom come, thy will be done on earth as it is in heaven.' This is our 'practice run' as it were. The time to work at getting it right, the time to be God's hands and feet, the time to act justly, love mercy and to walk humbly with our God, so that when we are called home we will hear, "Well done good and faithful servant," from our Lord and master Adonai.

**Prayer:** *Father, You have satisfied our desire for eternity through the death and resurrection of Jesus. You have proved over and over again what a good Shepherd You are. Adonai, You now challenge us to be a mirror of Your goodness. Such a challenge! Father we are up for it, because we want to see You glorified in our homes, communities and nations. This is our prayer in the name of Jesus our Risen King.*

Amen

# PART THREE

## Prose to Ponder

# Waiting for God?

Speaking with a cousin one day, she said, "Sometimes, don't you wish God would just pull up a chair and explain to us what He wants us to do, and where He wants us to go, rather than us having to work so hard to decipher what it is He is telling us?" This was the start of a conversation which we have revisited on several occasions.

I think we've all been in that place where we are trying to fathom a clear understanding, when we know we don't have all the information. It's rather like trying to complete a puzzle without the picture; you want the satisfaction of completing the puzzle and you are desperate to put it together to enjoy the result. So how would you tackle the puzzle in this situation? Well you may:

- Choose to hunt for the cover before laying a piece
- Work with the available puzzle pieces to buld it methodically and logically
- If it's a puzzle you have done before, you might decide to trust your memory and try to go for it confidently regardless
- You may give up because the task is so great it overwhelms you

Whichever option you choose, you will have varying degrees of success. And so it is with our Christian journey; our attitude to finding God's will determines our success and the degree of intimacy with God that we get from our faith.

God sees the whole picture and He reveals it to us a little at a time as we make ourselves available to the promptings of the Holy Spirit. This reliance on God is how we grow in our faith. So, let's examine each approach and see how it might add to our understanding of God, His presence and His plan for our lives.

Start a hunt for the cover:

You might decide to put your efforts into finding the picture of the puzzle and refuse to start without knowing what you are working towards, or what you are creating. There is a natural urge to have all the information, but sadly, it's easy to get preoccupied with that search and lose interest in, or deny yourself the joy of doing the puzzle, because you refuse to work with the pieces you have until you find the picture, and can see the whole puzzle for yourself.

This view has parallels with the Christian's walk. Sometimes we can become so obsessed with what we don't know about God's plan, that we fail to take that step of faith with the information He has given us. In the Parable of The Talents found in Matthew 25:14-30, one of the stewards entrusted with his master's resources decided to hide it away. When we are uncertain about our calling, we do not take a chance to use the gift that God has given us and see where it takes us. We wait instead for our calling to be dramatically revealed, and so risk missing out on the experience to go deeper with God, by simply trusting Him. We know that God is faithful and that He protects and provides for us, but we allow ourselves to become spiritually paralysed and unable to move forward in our faith.

God is the great 'I AM' – the God of the present – and if our gaze is away from the area where God is working in our lives, we miss experiences that could become testimonies to nurture our souls and the souls of others. Our spiritual temperature may dip until it becomes tepid or even cold. In short, our preoccupation with obtaining the full picture – despite knowing that God has all the pieces, holds the master picture and we should trust Him – can deprive us of the depth of joy and pleasure He wants us to experience as we grow closer to Him and learn to trust Him in all circumstances.

Work methodically and logically with what you have:

You start with certain basic truths, that straight edges must be the boundary of the puzzle and grooves of a particular shape can only accommodate specific pieces. You patiently study each piece because even in completing the edge it won't be immediately apparent where each piece fits.

Our basic truths are God's promises, so we say to the Lord, "In you, O Lord, I put my trust and I will not be put to shame," and with each step of trusting comes a clearer picture of God's plan for us and His purpose for our lives. We patiently study His word; we say "I trust You, tell me to come, and I'll walk to You." Like Peter, we can start walking on spiritual water towards all that God has in store for us. As we more closely study His Word, align ourselves with the truth of His Word, and delve deeper, we receive information to complete the picture one step at a time. His Holy Spirit speaks to us; and in this journey we realise that even the smallest step is significant, and our confidence to begin creates a space, where God can use us for His glory.

God wants us to be confident in our walk because He knows that the sense of gratification and spiritual fulfilment does not come from simply being told the answers. In fact, it comes from the experience of finding and walking in obedience to His will. Moreover, which child readily, happily and unquestioningly obeys a parent's direct instruction? If they do, it can be in a somewhat grudging way, and that is not the kind of obedience God requires or expects. God knows (and we have evidence from Adam and Eve's taking of the fruit in the Garden of Eden) that direct instruction does not always appear to work with us. He knows how to keep us engaged, to keep us wanting more and more of Him; He knows us better than we know ourselves!

Trust your memory and just go for it!

If you've done the puzzle before, then you have the advantage of 'muscle memory'. You are likely to recall particularly difficult parts, especially if it took a lot of effort to solve! That pain is well engrained in your memory so you recognise those tricky pieces and start building that part of the puzzle, while also working through the easier parts. With each piece you place, you are taking a chance, and if a piece doesn't fit, you know you will eventually find the correct piece.

Rather than God spoon-feeding us solutions, we can look

back in our life to see the pattern of God's goodness, mercy and faithfulness. During times of hardship, we remind ourselves that we serve a God who, unlike us, does not change. He was faithful then, and will be faithful now. Memories of God's faithfulness are the foundational backdrop for managing new challenges. We step out where we feel 'Spirit-led' and even if we misjudge this, we don't worry, because that step is already in God's amazing picture.

Do you remember the children of Israel crossing Jordan? They were asked to take stones and set them up as a memorial. Our testimonies are memorials that inspire us to 'go for it!' But we shouldn't allow the past to rob us of the moment, or the movement of God in our lives at the present time. The three disciples on the mount of transfiguration wanted to stay and worship, but Jesus had other plans for them. He wanted to move them into a different experience of, and with, the Father.

Our past can and should inform the present, but it is a small part on the continuum of the Christian journey and we should not linger there for too long. In over-staying, we risk missing out on new experiences and testimonies, and thereby fail to grow deeper in our relationship with God. As a result, we become ill equipped for the Christian walk of faith.

Give up because the task is overwhelming:

Ok, so you've looked everywhere and still can't find the picture. You become frustrated and irritable then put the puzzle away for another time when you might feel more inclined to have another go. Soon you forget about the puzzle or the pleasure it would have brought.

We may find ourselves at this place at some point in our Christian walk. We are just not sure if we are hearing from God. Whether it is the Holy Spirit, or is it simply our wishful thinking? How do we know it is God? How can we be sure? With these conflicting and confusing messages being sent to our brain, we may simply resort to our comfortable, default Christian existence. We may go through the motions of being a Christian, or not even do that much. We don't bother with cell groups, Christian fellowship and other opportunities to grow our faith – even attending the church services becomes an effort.

We want a direct answer from God and we stop engaging with Him when that answer doesn't come as we expect. When we worship, we do not access the depth of the Christian experience that the Father wants us to enjoy, and instances of God's past goodness and favour in our lives get lost beneath clouds of self-doubt and confusion. Sadly, because we haven't used what we have to engage with God, our Christian journey and faith growth is halted. We become like Elijah who, running scared and desperate to hear from God, became overwhelmed by the situation  he found himself in. But God, whose timing is always perfect, shows up right at his point of need, reminding him in that still small voice that he was not alone.  He was fed and refreshed for the next part of his journey.

The wonderful thing about the Father is that He understands our weaknesses and the lack-lustre way in which we sometimes engage. We have all probably spent hours worrying about what appeared a huge problem but which in the end came to nothing. In fact, we allowed the attitude to the problem to become greater than the problem itself. It is during these times, when it all becomes too much for us to bear, we need to say, "Lord, I believe I can do this, please help my unbelief."

Realistically, the answer to the question posed at the start is likely to be a bit of each. We spend a certain amount of time looking for the picture, but there comes a time to get started with the truths and promises God gives us. As we do this, we may remember testimonies which can strengthen our resolve and focus; we may need to stop for the day, not give up, but praise and worship and then resume the next day refreshed and equipped. Indeed, the Lord tells us that it is not by might or power, but only by His Spirit.

*'I will instruct you and teach you in the way you should go. I will guide you with My eye.'  (Psalm 32:8)*

# Passing the Baton

My favourite track sport as a teenager was the relay race and my preference was to run a middle leg. I did not like to start or end the race – possibly because I felt there was greater pressure in those positions. I soon realised, that every position was significant because if the baton did not make it to the end of the race, we would not qualify, let alone be 'winners,' irrespective of how fast each runner was.

Some of us now find ourselves living in a season where the years behind us are greater than those before us. At this time, we may take note of our frailties and perhaps begin to plan for our demise. We try to make the most of the time we feel we have left so that when we die, not only is the task for those we leave behind made easier, but perhaps more importantly, we leave resources and most importantly we leave behind a set of positive values from which others can benefit.

It is vitally important to the spiritual, physical and emotional health of the next generation that our value system forms the core of our baton, so our baton which is built of layers comprising Love, Integrity, Faith and Prayer, is securely held and transparently obvious. Furthermore, our value system needs to be accessible in a way which engages, by raising questions in the minds of those looking on – especially our young – and inspires them to keep going. The apostle Paul in Philippians 3:14 speaks of this, by telling us that he 'presses on to take hold.' He presents a racing analogy to us and we can visualise his focus and sheer determination to win his race.

Our young people are growing up in a very different reality from the one some of us grew up in. In their own way they are trying to make sense of the world. Without community and support from their family, they may find themselves drifting aimlessly and are therefore more than happy to attempt any attractive-looking proposition on offer. That is why it is so vitally important to pass on a set of values to our young so that they are well equipped for their life journey.

A central component of the baton that we need to get securely into the hands of the next generation is LOVE. It is no coincidence that in 1 Peter 4:8 the Bible says, '… Most of all love each other as if your life depended on it. Love makes up for practically anything'. (MSG)

1 Corinthians 13:4-8 is popular with Christians and non-Christians and is the number one most widely used marriage scripture and unarguably the best exhortation of love. Our relationship with God is affirmed by His love for us, and this love should affirm all our other relationships.

I often observe the way children greet their parents at the end of the school day because it tells me a lot about the atmosphere in the home. Some children race across the playground and literally throw themselves into the arms of waiting parents, whilst others drag themselves across the playground and are barely acknowledged by their parents, who are sometimes preoccupied with phone conversations. What signals are we as parents sending to those God has entrusted to our care?

Love starts in the home. Love is a value and appreciation that is not necessarily linked to our immediate feelings and as such, it transcends personal beliefs and is ever hopeful, always looking for the best in others. The love between parents and children is a pivotal one because it is from this love that a strong, healthy relationship is forged. Children get a sense of security and affirmation as they learn to take risks in a secure setting.

They learn to value themselves and gain a better understanding of who they are. As they receive love, they are better positioned to see and accept the love of the wider family members, resulting in the enhancement of their self-respect, positive self-esteem, and assured self-confidence. Love is like the navigation system through which we view the world and respond to it. It provides the emotional muscle our children need in a sometimes demanding, confusing and conflicting world.

Integrity, the next component of the baton, has sadly been tainted by the world system, which is underpinned by bitesize messages of self-importance and individualism where the mantra becomes "It's all about me," and "I'm worth it."

Jesus demonstrated integrity when He lived on earth by the way He treated those around Him. He did not treat people differently because they were richer, more sinful in the eyes of onlookers, came from His hometown, or even because they were a conquering power.

Integrity is difficult to define and it is one of those words we can sometimes use flippantly. The dictionary defines it as 'having strong moral principles' or 'the state of being whole.' I guess in layman's terms integrity is best defined as a behaviour that doesn't change depending on who we are with, or where we find ourselves.

A person of integrity is one who deals honestly and seeks to live by a strong moral code. In today's world that may seem anachronistic, as truth seems to no longer be an absolute but rather a changeable abstract. When Jesus was questioned 2000 years ago by Pilate, He said 'Everyone who is of the truth hears my voice.' Pilate immediately, almost dismissively, responded with 'What is truth?' suggesting that truth can be relative and may carry different shades of meaning, which can vary for different people.

The aspect of integrity we should be passing on is that truth is an absolute. We need to speak and live the truth even when it is difficult to do so. We need, however, to show that we are not cardboard cut-outs but people who encounter difficulties and sometimes struggle to line our faith up with the harsh realities of life. We will get things wrong as we make judgment calls as to how best to deal with these challenges. Integrity, however, should be our default setting – our personal internal check – so that onlookers are seeing a general consistency in the way we behave, as we demonstrate to those around us – especially the young – a  model of Christian living which sends out powerful life messages.

Our third baton component is FAITH. The Bible tells us that 'without faith it is impossible to please God.' Faith is a difficult concept, both to unpick in a practical sense and to identify outside of a religious context. We can rattle off the Bible verse 'Faith is the substance of things hoped for, the evidence of things not seen.' As Christians, our faith journey might look like a graph of peaks and troughs, but even when we are in those valley places we learn to take God at His word, so that His power can be demonstrated in and through us. That is perhaps the essence of faith; trusting and holding on regardless, unswervingly as Paul puts in Hebrews 10:23, knowing and believing with all our heart that God will come through for us.

To take God at His word though, we must know the living Word. It is this knowledge of the Word which informs our thought processes and directs our actions, thus sending a clear message to a younger generation, as they see our faith demonstrated through words and actions regardless of circumstances. From this, we can see that faith is not a stagnant concept, it is a live, dynamic, organic force, which drives us to make choices about how we live, and how we respond to situations, so that we can make a difference wherever we find ourselves.

The final component of the baton is PRAYER. Where would we be without prayer? Prayer opens up a doorway to Heaven for us. It is the link through which the Holy Spirit joins us to the throne room and allows us, through Jesus, to have access to God. The disciples urged Jesus to teach them how to pray because they must have seen something in Jesus that they needed – a very close relationship with the Father.

How then in a practical way, do we pass this on to the next generation, so that a passion and deep love of prayer becomes habit forming? When I was a child, my grandmother would wake us up at 5 a.m. for family devotions before our work or school day started. Some people do not go out of their front doors without a prayer or start the car before praying. Sometimes prayer needs to be in the quiet place, just you and God, but it also needs to take place in a space where others can see and feel it happening. Young people need to see that prayer is not confined to the church building, but it is a way of life. In prayer they see our vulnerabilities and our reliance on God. They see us sharing moments of pain and of joy with God.

Sometimes I find myself saying almost apologetically, "all I can do is pray", as though prayer is a last resort when in fact it should be our first course of action. The idea that prayer is the most important weapon in the Christian's arsenal needs to be reiterated repeatedly, and the young need to see that happening powerfully in the home.

These four components to our baton – LOVE, INTEGRITY, FAITH and PRAYER – of course do not exist in isolation. Like the runners in a relay race who form the team and the baton is passed smoothly from one to the next, these components are so interlinked that it is often difficult to see where one ends and another takes over. Each one supports, extends, explains and exemplifies the others, proclaiming and demonstrating to a watching world a model of Christian living which says (without words), "Do as I do, live as I live, treat others the way I do."

As we navigate with LOVE, let's set our default to INTEGRITY, accelerate confidently with FAITH, arm ourselves with PRAYER and head towards our finishing line!

# Seeds of Hope are Growing

Well, we had to do a lot of waiting between 2020 and 2022. Waiting for the infection rates to go down; waiting to get back to normal and to start social interactions on a wider scale; waiting for the opportunity to start holidaying again, going to church again, going shopping, getting our hair and nails done or perhaps waiting for the chance to get back to work. We were simply waiting to get back to normal.

Slowly, but surely, we saw the opening up of many of the above but still the hungry jaws of COVID-19 demands more and more, and with its many variants, wants to persist.

'Up from the ashes of disaster grow the roses of success' is one of the songs from Chitty Chitty Bang Bang, which I love. Another song written by Brenton Brown and Ken Riley tells us that strength will rise as we wait upon the Lord. Both songs send out a message of hope during a time of waiting, and invite us to look beyond our present circumstances and look with confidence to the future, because that is what hope does for and to us. What good could we possibly visualise as coming out of the COVID-19 pandemic?

One of the lessons COVID-19 taught and is still teaching us, is how truly global we are. For some of us, when the outbreak first emerged in China in December 2019, we sympathised but went back to sleep. When it emerged in Italy and Spain we perhaps empathised, and because it was now in Europe and closer to home, we rubbed our eyes. We then saw the outbreak in the U.S. and sat up, stretched and braced ourselves, so that when it arrived here almost simultaneously, we became truly awake, realising, perhaps for the first time, that COVID-19 was no respecter of borders.

As it continued its rampage through our world, we began to recognise that we were one race – the human race – and it was us against COVID-19. It was no longer the Chinese, Italians, Spanish or Americans, it was us – the people of the world – so we began to come together, racing to find a possible vaccine, opening manufacturing plants to produce PPE equipment, volunteering on the front line. We used the pain of the pandemic to open our eyes to the value of community, nationally and internationally. The seed of hope was planted and had begun to take root.

We didn't have to wait too long for the green shoots of hope to slowly emerge. Every Thursday, thousands, perhaps millions, around the country clapped, banged, sang and raised funds, doing their bit to say thank you to carers, delivery drivers, cleaners, postmen, supermarket workers, teachers and the NHS. COVID-19 made us realise that we certainly were all in this together.

As we adjusted to being in 'lockdown' some people began to use the time in creative ways, and in doing so, became a blessing to others. We began to see the value of the silence, some heard the birds as they listened; we spent more time with families, parents became teachers, engaging in a range of activities, and the earth said "Thank you" as pollution levels fell.

We heard stories of people volunteering to work in food banks, to deliver medicines to those sheltering, shopping for elderly neighbours, working in call centres providing advice on a range of issues, which could so easily overwhelm, not to mention the funds raised by ordinary people who cared, and dared to make a difference. We began to understand what community meant – a coming together to support, engage and encourage. Sir Tom Moore, at the age of 99 (who has since sadly died), walking laps of his garden, spurred on others, old and young to do something similar, raising millions for our NHS.

People from different races, religions, age groups came together in a sense of unity and neighbourly love. People who had lived next to each other for many years and had never spoken came out to clap together and some have now forged lasting friendships. It has been such a powerfully beautiful picture, that for me, it has become my visual metaphor for hope. As it takes me back emotionally to Christ's love for us, I am reminded of the question asked of Jesus, "Who is my neighbour?"

COVID-19 rampaged through our world taking many lives in its sinister path, but like Paul, we can still say 'We are hard pressed on every side, but not crushed; perplexed, but not in despair, persecuted, but not abandoned; struck down but not destroyed'
(2 Corinthians 4:8-9).

Whilst I do not want to make light of the personal, agonising pain suffered by those who have lost friends and relatives, Christians know that victory comes through battle and after every trial when faced prayerfully, there is triumph. We often look for tangible evidence of triumph so that we can say for example, 'Yes, I received healing' or 'My child got through their exam' – the things we can point to that confirm to us, and others, that God has indeed been faithful. But you know, often the triumph is in how we deal with the trial and the lesson it teaches us individually and collectively.

Songs are one of my ways of being encouraged and when in 2012 the devastating news that I had breast cancer was delivered to me, one of the songs that kept me going was 'Blessings' by Laura Story, the chorus of which simply asks:

What if Your blessings come through raindrops?
What if Your healing comes through tears?
What if a thousand sleepless nights
Are what it takes to know You're near?
What if trials of this life are Your mercies in disguise?

The way communities around the world came together was a sure sign that hope was growing during a time of pain. As the branches of hope reached out and upwards in tentative expectation of an end to the pandemic, so too, as neighbours and community, we were reaching out to each other.

The pandemic overwhelmingly brought out the very best in us as we journeyed through the avalanche of pain and uncertainties in its path. What though, will be the lessons learnt from this experience when we finally emerge from the devastating clutches of this disease?  A disease that has shaken the very foundations of our economic, social, political and educational system, and has sent a tsunami of aftershocks into the very heart of society – not to mention the toll it has taken on all the emotional wellbeing of us all.

I am often disappointed by the cliché, so often voiced after serious incidents, that 'lessons will be learnt.'  The whispers in 2020-2021 of 'we will rebuild, we will get back to normal' became so urgent that we perhaps failed to reflect on the COVID-19 experience and simply launched ourselves into the continuation of the status quo. As we have a vaccine, we  simply carry on from where we left off, as though nothing happened.

So how can we rebuild and ensure that the delicate buds of hope are not strangled and left to wither by humanity's greed? I smiled to myself when, in 2020, I saw Cuban doctors going to Italy to help with the early epidemic there.  A so-called 'third world' country helping the 'first world'!

How then can we ensure that we do not lose sight of the selfless work done throughout that period and maintain that  sense of community which emerged out of our shared pain? How can we use this experience to address the glaring inequalities in society and our world? How will we harness the best in us, so that we get the best out of others, and as a result, build better communities, a better nation and a better world?

One of the tasks I give to my students when I meet them at the start of the academic year is to write a recipe for their model classroom. They often write something like this before going on to describe how each ingredient is going to be sifted, stirred, added generously etc:

**Ingredients:**
30 students and 2 adults
20 tablespoons of respect
500g of love
A sprinkle of tolerance and patience

Do you get the idea? These are 10 and 11 year-olds designing the classroom community they would like to be a part of!  We now have a chance to re-design our communities after COVID-19. What an opportunity! How will we respond and rise triumphantly from the ashes of COVID-19?

It is perhaps not a coincidence that the symbol chosen to show support and unity was the rainbow. For Christians, the rainbow offering hope was as a covenant sign from God to Noah and his family. We now have the privilege to covenant together as a community and nation to make decisions as to how, like the butterfly, we will emerge from our COVID-19 cocoon and allow the leaves of hope to flourish in the winds of time. Just as Greta Thunberg, a sixteen year-old school girl, championed the cause of climate change, so too can each individual – though a drop in the ocean – champion the case for a fairer world where love, integrity and respect for all is woven into the fabric of politics and policies. It starts with us, in our communities where God has placed us for such a time as this.

# Going Through the Fire and into the Promise

I don't know what giants you are facing, what difficulties you are going through or indeed the mountains you have to climb. But one thing I know and feel qualified to share with you is that God is good, God is able, God is willing, and God will see you through. Remember Daniel's friends, three were thrown into the fire, but four were seen and the fourth was the Lord who was with His faithful servants.

As you stand on the brink of your new tomorrow, remember the spies sent in to evaluate the territory of Canaan, and be like Caleb and Joshua who did not give in to doubt and fear. I urge you to stand firm on the promises of God and what He has spoken concerning you.

Well-wishers fall into two broad categories: those who encourage through acts of kindness and supportive words, and those whose mission it is to 'educate' you about your situation.

When I was diagnosed, I was very selective about whom I shared the information with. One day someone I hadn't told, called me and proceeded to tell me about how many family members we had lost to cancer. I recognised that she wasn't being unkind, she simply did not appreciate that the peace I was demonstrating in my situation was a rather fragile one.

I remember organising my desk as I would not be in school for the spring term when a colleague came to say goodbye. After she left, the thought came over me, "Actually yes, this really could be goodbye." The only thing I could do in that situation was to hold on to the promises of God. Some powerful people had prayed over my life, and I felt that God gave me this promise: "You will live to see your grandchildren." I held tightly to that promise, and as I prepared for the reality of my situation I also knew that God was my ultimate reality and, like the Hebrew children, He would see me through.

We must trust God and take those faltering steps even when the ground is shaky. We must look beyond our circumstances and up in anticipation of God's blessings. I must confess after the birth of my first grandchild in 2017, I did say to God something like, "You said grandchildren right?" My second grandchild was born in 2019!

I can't promise that all your financial problems will be solved, or that you will get that dream job, that your relationships will always go smoothly, or indeed that you will never experience health issues. The simple fact is, we live in a broken world. What I can say to you is this: Do not let challenges hem you in, do not let fear take a hold, do not let the opinion of others steal your joy and peace but instead remember that nothing can separate us from the love of God which is in Christ Jesus (Romans 8:38-39) and that we move forward with Christ no matter what.

As you stand on the brink of your new tomorrow and survey your 'promised land' there will be challenges between where you are now, and what you are moving into. The amazing thing is that God has already gone ahead and scouted out the territory! He has put things in place to alleviate some of the pain, so remind yourself of the great God that you serve and step out in faith to receive. I promise you, that waiting on the other side is a stronger and more confident person of faith – you!

*'When you pass through the waters, I will be with you and when you pass through the rivers, they will not sweep over you. When you walk through the fire, you will not be burned; the flames will not set you ablaze'. (Isaiah 43:2)*

# A Conversation We Must Have

'First they came for the socialists and I did not speak out because I was not a socialist. Then they came for the trade unionists and I did not speak out because I was not a trade unionist. Then they came for the Jews and I did not speak out because I was not a Jew. Then they came for me and there was no one left to speak for me.'

*Martin Niemoller, German pastor and critic of Hitler (1892-1984)*

Would the Holocaust have happened had the world spoken out about the enslavement of millions of Africans between the 17th-19th century?

I would like to believe that the answer would be an emphatic no! Answers however, as we know have varying shades of grey and are therefore rarely that simple.

When the slogan 'Black Lives Matter' first arrived on the public platform, I confess I was one of those who thought, *If only they added 'too'* at the end of the phrase, because let's face it, every life matters. As I contemplated this, I questioned whether there was a time in history when all people enjoyed the same respect. I questioned whether, if prior to enslavement, colonialism and empire building days, black lives were valued, and then wondered at which point the paradigm shift might have occurred, which caused black lives to seemingly matter less.

With such considerations as our backdrop, as well as the experience of many black people today, we exclaim in anger, "Black lives matter!" We protest, set up forums to debate it, have reports commissioned, written and then perhaps shelved. Alternatively, we can ask the question, then have an open, honest conversation, starting perhaps with why such a slogan is needed in the twenty-first century.

One of the things which I admired about Nelson Mandela was the urgency with which he set up the Truth and Reconciliation Commission in South Africa, so that between 1995 and 2003, victims of apartheid and those who had supported the system could talk openly about their experiences. The Commission was not set up to bring people to justice or even indeed to raise issues of reparation, but simply to give people an opportunity to talk about a lived experience, whatever side of the divide they found themselves on.

In our society today there are people – Christians and non-Christians, black and white – who feel aggrieved at the way Africans were stripped of their humanity and subsequently treated during the period of enslavement. There is also a strong sense of injustice at the way the continent was carved up and dished out to Europeans in the nineteenth century, and at how even today, the contributions made by Africa and Africans on the world stage are so very often ignored. I believe it is partly this denial of the contributions of Africans which has led to the devaluing of the African people. The arrogance and ignorance of Europeans looking at the Benin Bronzes and remarking that they must have been crafted by non-Africans!

So, let's briefly have a look at Africa's history. It is well documented – though less well known generally as it is not taught in schools – that Africa enjoyed a long period of stability with advances in technology, medicine, mathematics and astronomy. Some have even argued that the ancient Greeks learnt from the Africans and took this knowledge back to Greece.

During the Middle Ages when Europe was a relatively backward continent, empires in Mali, Ghana and Songhay expanded. The first Hausa city states were emerging in Nigeria as was the Kingdom of Benin from about AD 900. The great Zimbabwe was constructed somewhere between AD 1200 and AD 1400 and the great African ruler Mansa Musa had a vast empire across West Africa.

From this evidence, we can see that Africa is not the 'dark uncivilised continent' it was made out to be. We therefore need to ask ourselves why it is, that in the history of world civilization, Africa is only just beginning to be recognised. Why did those who wrote 'world history' choose, for such a long time, to omit Africa and the contributions of Africans?

Ancient Egypt unified under Menes in 3100 B.C. is often seen as the first of Africa's great kingdoms. It would appear that ancient Egypt just happened, as there is no reference to the earlier Nubian kingdom of Ta Seti, which many believe was the starting point for African history.
It is this lack of continuity in history which frustrates me at times. It is as though history should be taught as a list of

specific events unrelated to events before and after. I have often asked myself how children can be taught about the Industrial Revolution and the Victorians without talking and teaching about the enslavement of Africans, when the cotton mills of Northern England were fueled by the cotton picked in the states of Southern America.

In an effort therefore to develop a history curriculum which reflected the black presence in the United Kingdom over time, I set about researching how black people were presented pre and post colonialism.

In this piece, I hope to identify a starting point when black lives were perhaps first regarded as worthless, the strategies which were put in place to support and reinforce such a view, then briefly summarise the legacy of enslavement, and identify ways in which education in the widest sense, could be used as an effective tool to address this issue.

One of the earliest records of the history of black people in Britain was that of the 'Ivory Bangle Lady' found in York in 1901. She died in the 4th century, and it is suggested that she was of mixed heritage, perhaps from North Africa. From the items found in her stone coffin, it appears that she was probably quite a wealthy and respected woman.

With the Roman invasion of Britain in 43 A.D. solders from all over the Roman Empire arrived in Britain. Between AD 253 and AD 258 Hadrian's Wall was guarded by an African division of Roman soldiers (Aurelian Moors) stationed near Carlisle. Being a citizen of Rome conferred many privileges, and it was of little consequence which part of the Empire you came from initially, or indeed the colour of your skin. Those soldiers arriving in Britain would probably have had their families with them and living as part of the community.

In an abbreviated version of the Domesday Book of 1211 there is an image of a black Briton. The records give no indication as to how these people were treated and one could argue, that their inclusion in accounts suggests that they were accepted as part of the community.

During Tudor times, William Dunbar in one of his poems appear to be referring to an African woman in a pageant in Scotland. There is also evidence of the presence of black people in London and at the court of Henry VII and Henry VIII. John Blanke was a black musician living in London in 1507 and records show that he was paid much more than the average servant at the time. This would suggest that he was not being exploited because of colour, but was recognised and valued as a musician.

Other black people in Tudor England included Jacques Francis, a diver who collected many of the guns from the sunken Tudor ship, *The Mary Rose*. There are church records of other black people like Mary Ellis, a seamstress, who lived in Britain and was baptised into the Christian faith. These people were often servants who married and had their own families.

At some point during the reign of Elizabeth I, the tide seemed to have shifted and the prevailing opinion about Africans became negative. The increase in numbers (many of the new arrivals were slaves captured from Spanish ships in the ongoing war with the British) and not being Christians appeared to have been the driving force behind the change in attitudes.

In 1555, the English merchant John Lok had brought a group of five Ghanaians to London in an effort to enlist support and help from them by teaching them English and using them as interpreters in Africa. This visit provided an opportunity for Londoners to encounter Africans, and to hopefully dispel some of the myths about Africa and Africans, which were being circulated by explorers and other travellers. Stories that Africans were carefree, inferior, lazy and cannibals however continued to circulate.

It is interesting to note that, when approached by John Hawkins to sanction the slave trade and compete with Portugal, Queen Elizabeth I at first warned that '...carrying off Africans without their consent would be detestable and would bring down the vengeance of heaven.' It was not long, however, before she was persuaded that it 'would be good for the souls of Africans' and it would also, of course, bring great economic wealth to Britain.

The myths about Africa, referred to earlier, came into their own in the early seventeenth century when British plantations were established in the Americas. Since it was believed that Africans were inferior to 'civilised' Europeans, kidnapping and forced labour were easily sanctioned.

Noteworthy is the fact that in the early 17th century, North America was becoming populated by the first English colonists, the Pilgrim Fathers, a strict protestant sect, who chose to leave Britain in order to worship freely. Just over a century later, after the War of Independence, when the Founding Fathers drafted the new constitution, they ensured that amendments written into the 'Bill of Rights' stated that the rights of individual people and the state were respected unless those people were slaves, or Native Americans. These were Christian leaders!

By the middle of the seventeenth century, the economic system of trading in slaves developed by the Portuguese, was further built on by the British and French and it was not long before there were plantations across the Caribbean and America. The new gold (sugar-cane) provided a lucrative income so that by 1698 the enslavement of Africans became an assumed right for the English and other Europeans.

It would appear then, that sometime possibly during the mid 16th century, Africa and Africans were rebranded in such a way as to make them easily exploitable. Readers, I am hoping that you can see how preconceptions and misconceptions give rise to negative ideas that germinate and grow, and how like cancer, their tentacles reach down the centuries with negative consequences, because they have been used to support policies which have since served to marginalize groups of people. This marginalisation of groups whether through antisemitic practice, sexism or blatant racism is clearly an issue of injustice, and needs to be responded to accordingly.

For centuries black lives had little meaning beyond being a valuable commodity. In Britain, there were slaves working in the homes of the aristocracy as well as in the homes of others, and it was regarded as a mark of status. The brutal reality of life as a slave was generally hidden from the English population and the prevailing opinion appears to have been that enslavement was a way of civilising Africans and teaching them about God, therefore it was an acceptable thing to do.

As the English 'buried their heads in the sand' about what was happening in the colonies new scientific ideas were emerging to support the view of the 'inferior African.' The birth of eugenics and Darwin's theory of evolution had the scientific community convinced that evolution was a fact. The plethora of images which were used to illustrate this theory, gave further credence to the African as being an inferior being. Coupled with eugenics and ideas that there were different races of man, many Europeans condoned enslavement as it was supported and legitimised (some may argue) by science. In an 18th century European map of Africa, the western region is shown and the coastline divided into four zones which are labelled 'grain', 'ivory', 'gold' and 'slave coast.'

With the passing of the Abolition Act in 1833 and the realisation that slavery was becoming uneconomical, European powers turned their attention to the lucrative resources that Africa held. Within about fifty years after the abolition of slavery in Britain, at a conference of European leaders in 1885 and working from a map five metres tall, the continent of Africa was divided up between the thirteen invited nations without any thought being given for the people who lived there or indeed for its history. A few years later the City of Benin was burnt and its artifacts taken. It is also worth noting here, that slave owners were compensated for their loss with the abolition of slavery, whilst those who had been enslaved have not received a penny to this day!

When we fast forward to events in the twentieth and twenty-first century, we can see how past events continue to fuel conditions and experiences for particular groups of people. That is why we need to look back, to understand the present. So here we are today chanting the slogan 'Black Lives Matter!'

Dangerous ideas have dangerous consequences and we are living with those consequences all over the world. We see them manifested in the relative 'poverty' of Africa and the Caribbean, in the limited life chances of people of colour (housing, education, mental health, employment). In the U.K. we see the hostile environment which the Windrush generation is caught up in, and we see it being played out on the streets in the culture of gang violence which is draining the life blood of communities.

Wrong assumptions clearly led to wrong conclusions. We can perhaps see that now, but those assumptions seem to have been engraved into the psyche. In 1906 Ota Benga, a pygmy, was exhibited in a cage in Bronx Zoo and in 2020, Amy Cooper, a white woman, falsely accused a black man of threatening her, telling him that she was going to tell the police that an African American man was following her. She felt comfortable doing that because she knew who the police were likely to believe. We see a policeman in 2020 kneeling on the neck of George Floyd in the U.S.! The murder of Stephen Lawrence in London in 1993 also serves as an example of how little black lives are respected. These examples epitomise prevailing attitudes in some quarters and serve to illustrate that there is still a long way to go before we can truly appreciate that all lives matter.

As a Christian, how do I reconcile the past with the present and where is God in all of this? Just like the Holocaust in the twentieth century, the enslavement of Africans was a vile sin. Events like these clearly demonstrate what happens when people move away from God's template. God created one race – the human race – but others have sought to redefine God's perfect creation and in doing so have created sub-classes of people in order to justify their own selfishness and greed, when in reality, all are made in God's image.

I believe there are two key institutions – the Church and schools – which must lead on this if we are to appreciate that all lives matter.

The established Church sanctioned enslavement by the keeping of slaves and benefitted greatly from slave labour. In all of this, we recognise and applaud the work done by Christians such as William Knibb, Josiah Wedgewood and William Wilberforce. We know that in all the colonies black people led revolts to bring slavery to an end.

It is time for the Church to recognise the ills of the past and to publicly seek God's forgiveness. It cannot pretend that enslavement happened such a long time ago, that we should just move on, or that by paying 'lip service' and making shallow apologies, the situation has been addressed. I am not advocating that we live in the past, rather that we acknowledge the past as a severe stain on our history, seek forgiveness and make attempts to redress the wrong. I am not even advocating reparation as a first response, I am saying that we must talk about it. I believe that the Church is uniquely placed to be a voice for change. I acknowledge and respect those who argue that the Church should not involve itself in politics and to those I simply say that politics is all around us and Jesus spoke up when the politics of religious leaders led to injustice or blinded others to God's love.

I believe that many young people are turned away from the Church because they find an imbalance with Christianity, because of the past and present behaviour of the Church. I believe it is only through dialogue that this can be truly addressed. It does not matter how much we protest – if we do not acknowledge what happened, it is impossible to challenge and change the prevailing view.

Should the British National Curriculum in the twenty-first century address the divisive consequence of enslavement, and although a negative aspect of British history, include it nonetheless? Most certainly yes! Children need to be taught, so that they understand that history is not simply a list of dates, or events from the past. They need to see a connection between the past and the present. We need to be careful though, that our teaching is balanced, and acknowledges the fact that the abolition of slavery came about as a result of the efforts of Europeans as well as Africans, and that the enslaved did not just passively accept their lot. Individuals like Olaudah Equano, Toussant l'Overture, William Knibb and many others gave their voice and sometimes their lives to the abolition of slavery.

Children need to know that in their own way they are history-makers, and that whatever the issue, whether it be climate change, injustice or indeed a pandemic, their response to it today will constitute the history studied by future generations. When history is taught through the eyes of all involved, both sides of the story will be told, and only then will the truth of the past be revealed as we present a balanced curriculum to all our children based – in this instance – on the truth and pain of enslavement.

In her book 'Learning Beyond the Objective in Primary Education', Ruth Wills a music teacher in Lancashire, England, writes about our capacity to connect with ourselves, others and the world at a deeper level. She cites an example in one of her lessons where her students were singing songs from the Civil Rights Movement when one of the girls started to cry. A boy stood up and explained that his friend was crying because people were treated so badly and that it is the same today.

A conversation followed and when the lesson ended the boy said he would go home that night and tell people to stop being racist. Ruth describes this as being a transformational and emotional moment that went far beyond the learning objective for the lesson.

There are lots of opportunities for ensuring that our curriculum is truly inclusive. Black History Month was a great start but we need to now move beyond the month and find creative ways to make our curriculum truly inclusive. We need to ensure that all our children have:

- a true sense of their worth
- an appreciation of the contribution of Africa to civilisation
- access to the truth of history

The Bible says in John 8:32, 'You shall know the truth, and the truth shall make you free.' I do not believe that I am taking things out of context as I truly believe that Scripture is for teaching in all kinds of contexts. That is why it is a living Word to be applied to all of the circumstances of life.

I believe that the truth of the past will set us all free today in the present. When descendants of both those who condoned slavery and those who suffered under the system, face the uncomfortable truth that the grace of God was abused, we need to pray for His forgiveness and love so that we can move forward. As this happens, liberty and hope will be released. When we appreciate that our salvation – bought by the blood of Jesus – is a message of love and forgiveness, those wronged will recognise that Jesus forgave, so they too should forgive those who have wronged them.

It is time to have an honest and open conversation, a conversation which I believe the Church and schools should be spearheading. Until this happens, some of our children will continue to flounder in a wilderness of untruths and confusion. I've been accused of being a bit naïve, but I must live in hope and so I grasp at the threads of optimism: I celebrate everything positive which points to a change in how black people, particularly black children, are viewed. I celebrate every success and applaud and support those who work for a change.

I started this by asking a simple question but in reality this goes much wider than racism. This is about the heart of God, justice and a fairer society for all.

## References
*A History of the Black Presence in London (1966)*, Greater London Council
*Out of Slavery (2004)*, Nardia Foster
*Slavery and its Abolition (2007)*, Watford African Caribbean Association Black British History (2007), Oxford University Press
*Black and British a Forgotten History (2016)*, David Olusoga
*Black Tudors (2018)*, Miranda Kaufmann, Oneworld Publications
*Learning Beyond the Objective in Primary Education (2022)*, Ruth Wills, Routledge

# I Have a Dream

On 28th August 1963 Martin Luther King Jnr delivered his now famous ''I Have A Dream Speech' on the steps of the Lincoln Memorial in Washington D.C.

His speech was a cry from the heart to end the racism against black people that permeated American society. Today, there is another evil stalking our young here in Great Britain. As Christians, we know there is another way – God's way – and we pray and yearn for a move of His Holy Spirit in our communities.

Martin Luther King was a Baptist Minister and were he alive today and looking at the young casualties of knife and gun crimes in Great Britain, his cry from the heart speech, may have read something like this:

### *I have a dream today*

I have a dream that one day soon, here in London, we will see a change in our young people. Whereas before, killing with knives and guns was almost a daily occurrence, this will be replaced with a new sense of community togetherness, engendering positive self-esteem, dignity and a respect for life, knowing that God alone gives life, and He alone should take it.

## *I have a dream today*

I have a dream that as God gives us His vision for a new tomorrow, fear, anger and frustration will dissipate, and flags with messages of hope, forgiveness and togetherness will sway in the wind of love and reconciliation and His blanket of peace will overshadow our communities.

## *I have a dream today*

I have a dream that on the streets where blood has been so readily spilt, works of art depicting and reflecting love and acceptance will blossom, flower and flourish.

## *I have a dream today*

I have a dream that our young will grasp opportunities to thrive and be the best they can be, that communities will no longer wake up to the daily nightmare which ominously stalks some of our young, shrouding them with a cloak of immorality.

## *I have a dream today*

I have a dream that our young people will earnestly seek God and walk in the light of His love so that the violence which strikes terror into the hearts of our communities will be eradicated, and instead love, hope and healing will bubble and take root in our communities.

### I have a dream today

I have a dream that the God-centred values of love and justice will become the norm in our societies; that the injustices of hatred, poverty and lies will once and for all be eradicated, and that God's justice and freedom will reign, that the bells of engagement will ring out bringing a message of hope, reconciliation and peace.

### I have a dream today

I have a dream that individuals will live the African proverb which says, "It takes a village to raise a child"; that we will stand together in unity; being mothers, fathers, aunties, uncles, brothers, sisters and grandparents; that we will value and nurture every child as though they were our very own.

### I have a dream today.

*This piece of writing came about because of a discussion with my Year 6 class. We had been speaking to the children about transition to secondary school and that conversation ballooned into a conversation about different issues. Some children shared concerns about climate change, racism, gender inequalities but overwhelmingly the concerns were about drugs, and knife and gun crimes, and about how unsafe they felt about travelling to and from school. I wrote a variation of this as* a template for them to use for their own 'I Have A Dream Speech.' And what they wrote opened my eyes to their hearts.

As a result, in 2019 some friends and I set up a group called Esther 4:14 where we committed ourselves to meet weekly and pray for our young people.

'Yet who knows whether you have come to the kingdom for such a time as this?' (Esther 4:14)

*Pauline's work will appeal to, and inspire, a wide readership because of the way she sensitively narrates in prose and poems her life's journey with acceptance, endurance, humility and compassion, grounded in her strong Christian values and beliefs.*

*One can sense her positivity, the joys and challenges she experienced in childhood years and in adulthood as mother, teacher, grandmother, and friend. The "Why me?" became the "Why not me?" as her Christian faith strengthened.*

*The narratives provide a platform for the reader to reflect on similarities in their own life's ups and downs, simultaneously increasing awareness of how one could navigate a safe and comfortable path by putting God at the centre of their daily lives.*

*A genuinely insightful and pleasurable read...highly recommended to all regardless of social and religious beliefs.*

**Beverley Bogle**
**JANUKA Quadrille Group Coordinator**

# REFLECTIONS

# REFLECTIONS